THE
ACADEMIA
WALTZ
BY
BERKE BREATHED
(BĔRK' BRĔTH'-ED)

Sterling Swift Publishing company
ISBN 0-88408-122-2

Introductio

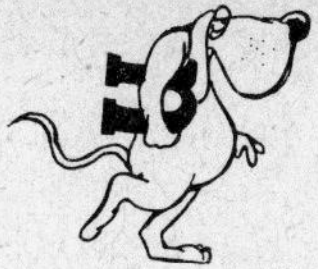

It's 8:30 a.m. one Monday some time ago. I've just answered the phone. I am butt naked, as that is how I normally sleep.

"Hello."

"Yes, is this Berkie Breethed?" (small feminine voice)

"Berke Breathed . . . but that was pretty close."

"You're the cartoonist?"

"That's right."

"Well, I just wanted to tell you that . . . um . . . that your cartoons aren't . . . um . . . any good."

"Oh. I'm sorry."

"Well that's all. Thank-you . . ."

"Wait a minute, (waking up) aren't you going to substantiate your comment?"

"What?"

"Explain yourself I mean. Do you call up Mario Puzo at 8:00 am in the morning when you don't like one of his books?"

"Look, you write about the same . . . um . . . things everyday. Frats, disco and sex, everyday."

"You don't approve of frats, disco and sex?"

"No. I mean yes . . . look, I think sex is just fine . . ."

"Me too. Say, did you know that I'm standing here butt naked?"

"You're *disgusting*."

"Look toots, (straightening) you want me to write about the crucial issues of today, right? The ones that people should be concerned with . . . ones of great importance, like the Nuke controversy . . ."

"EXACTLY."

"Fine. What can you tell me about it?"

"It's a greatly important issue."

"Anything else?"

"Look, I've got early classes. I don't have much time for reading the newspaper."

"Except for my cartoon . . ."

"Yes. But it's not any good."

"Mmm. Excuse me, I'm going back to bed now . . ."

"Hey . . . um . . . you're not thinking of putting me in your silly cartoon, are you?"

"Well, let's see. You're definately not in a fraternity, disco probably doesn't fit either . . . and a big NO in the sex category. Nope . . . looks like you'll be spared my poison pen."

"That's a relief."

"Fine. Well I'll just be off to bed now . . ."

"Wait."

"Mmm?"

"Um . . . look . . . uh, why wasn't I in the sex category?"

"Bad guess maybe. Say, did you know that I'm standing here butt naked?"

"(click)"

Berke Breathed
Austin, Texas
March 1979

To Grandfather,
Who's Offended By
Some And Laughs
At Few, But Who
Seems To Cherish
Them All

I
EARLY STUFF

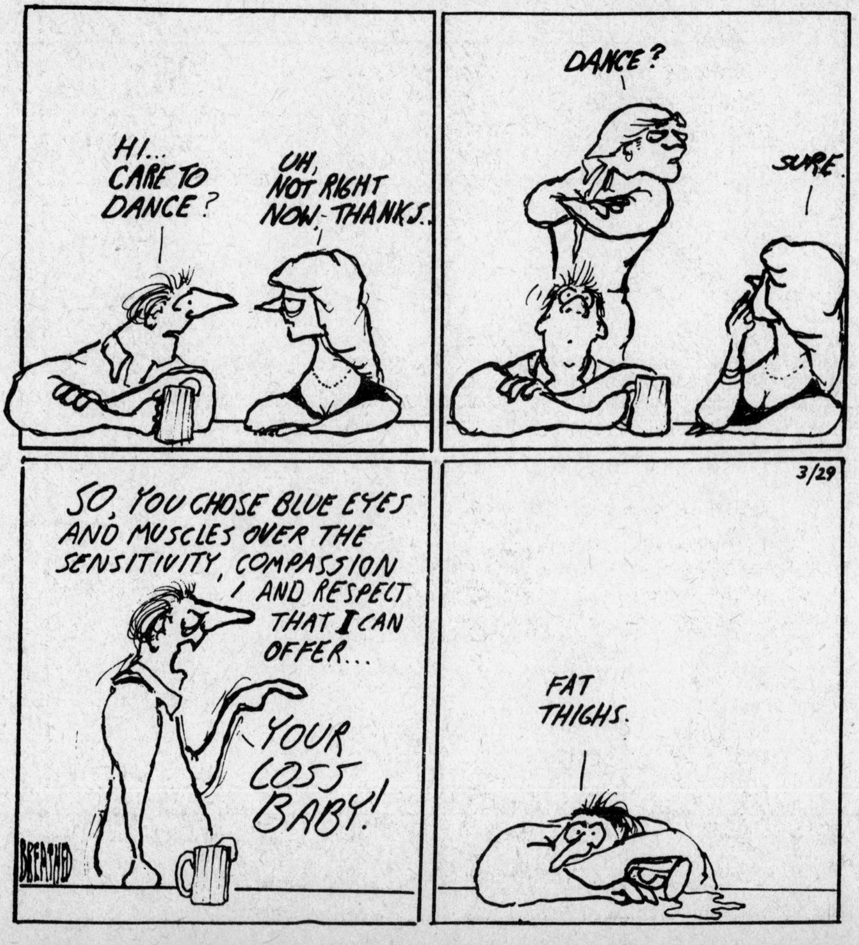
HI...
CARE TO
DANCE?
UH,
NOT RIGHT
NOW - THANKS...
DANCE?
SURE.
SO, YOU CHOSE BLUE EYES
AND MUSCLES OVER THE
SENSITIVITY, COMPASSION
AND RESPECT
THAT I CAN
OFFER...
YOUR
LOSS
BABY!
BREATHED
3/29
FAT
THIGHS.

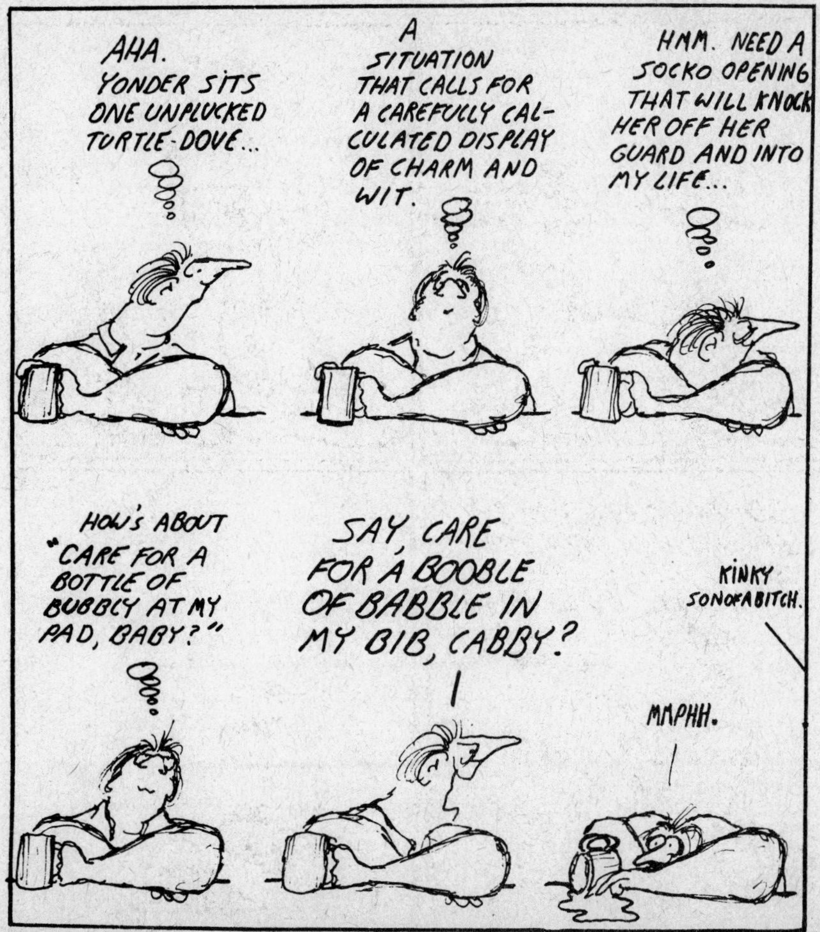
AHA. YONDER SITS ONE UNPLUCKED TURTLE-DOVE...
A SITUATION THAT CALLS FOR A CAREFULLY CAL-CULATED DISPLAY OF CHARM AND WIT.
HMM. NEED A SOCKO OPENING THAT WILL KNOCK HER OFF HER GUARD AND INTO MY LIFE...
HOW'S ABOUT "CARE FOR A BOTTLE OF BUBBLY AT MY PAD, BABY?"
SAY, CARE FOR A BOOBLE OF BABBLE IN MY BIB, CABBY?
KINKY SONOFABITCH.
MMPHH.

SAY HANDSOME, WHY DON'T WE GET TO KNOW EACH OTHER AT MY PLACE?
YOU'RE HUSTLING ME?
WELL, YOU DON'T HAVE TO PUT IT JUST THAT WAY.
CHRISESAKE, I'VE BEEN HAVING ROTTEN LUCK AT THIS DISCO FOR THREE DAYS, AND THEN SOME CUTE NUMBER LIKE YOU PUTS THE MOVE ON ME!!
UH.. HA, HA, I GUESS I DON'T EVEN KNOW YOUR NAME.
NORMAN. NICE TO MEETCHA.

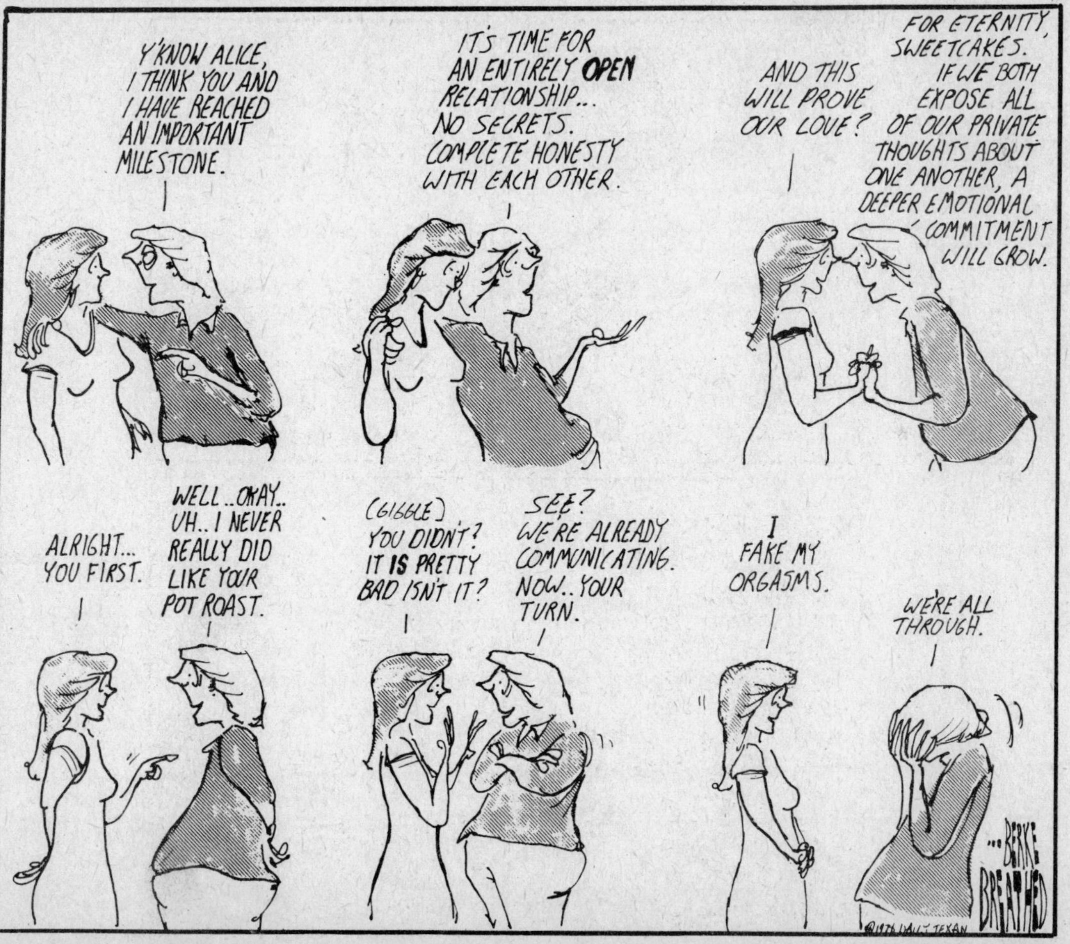
Y'KNOW ALICE, I THINK YOU AND I HAVE REACHED AN IMPORTANT MILESTONE.
IT'S TIME FOR AN ENTIRELY **OPEN** RELATIONSHIP... NO SECRETS. COMPLETE HONESTY WITH EACH OTHER.
AND THIS WILL PROVE OUR LOVE?
FOR ETERNITY, SWEETCAKES. IF WE BOTH EXPOSE ALL OF OUR PRIVATE THOUGHTS ABOUT ONE ANOTHER, A DEEPER EMOTIONAL COMMITMENT WILL GROW.
ALRIGHT... YOU FIRST.
WELL..OKAY.. UH.. I NEVER REALLY DID LIKE YOUR POT ROAST.
(GIGGLE) YOU DIDN'T? IT **IS** PRETTY BAD ISN'T IT?
SEE? WE'RE ALREADY COMMUNICATING. NOW.. YOUR TURN.
I FAKE MY ORGASMS.
WE'RE ALL THROUGH.
...BERKE BREATHED
©1976 DAILY TEXAN

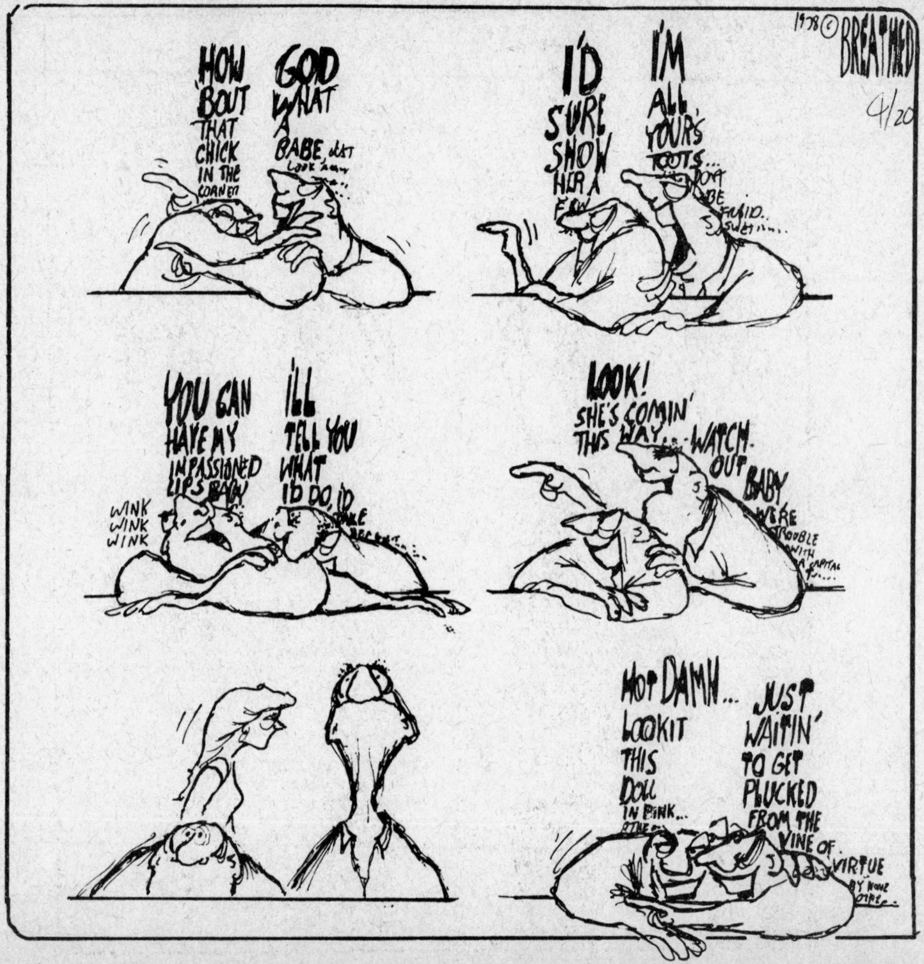
1978 © BREATHED
4/20
HOW 'BOUT THAT CHICK IN THE CORNER
GOD WHAT A BABE, JUST LOOK AT
I'D SURE SHOW HER A FEW
I'M ALL YOURS TOOTS... DON'T BE AFRAID.. SWEET.....
YOU CAN HAVE MY IMPASSIONED LIPS BABY
WINK WINK WINK
I'LL TELL YOU WHAT I'D DO, I'D TAKE
LOOK! SHE'S COMIN' THIS WAY..
WATCH OUT BABY
WE'RE TROUBLE WITH A CAPITAL T....
HOT DAMN... LOOKIT THIS DOLL IN PINK...
JUST WAITIN' TO GET PLUCKED FROM THE VINE OF VIRTUE

WELL GLORIA, WE'VE BEEN SEEING ALOT OF EACH OTHER LATELY... AND UH... WELL, HOW DO YOU FEEL ABOUT COMING HOME WITH ME TONIGHT?
I THINK I WOULD LIKE THAT..
YOU WOULD? I... OH, THATS NICE... IT IS NICE, ISN'T IT?
OF COURSE SILLY..
HMM.. UH, GEE.., I DON'T KNOW QUITE HOW TO ASK THIS...
DON'T BE COY...
WELL... IT'S SORT OF NONE OF MY BUSINESS... BUT THEN IT SORT OF IS TOO...
C'MON, I'LL UNDER-STAND.
UM... ER.. ARE YOU ON THE PILL?
WELL, YES, I AM.
OH HEY, I'M REALLY GLAD WE CAN BE HONEST AND OPEN WITH EACH OTHER WITHOUT SACRIFICING DIGNITY OR RESPECT.
ME TOO.
SO OBVIOUSLY YOUR SLEEPING AROUND QUITE A BIT...

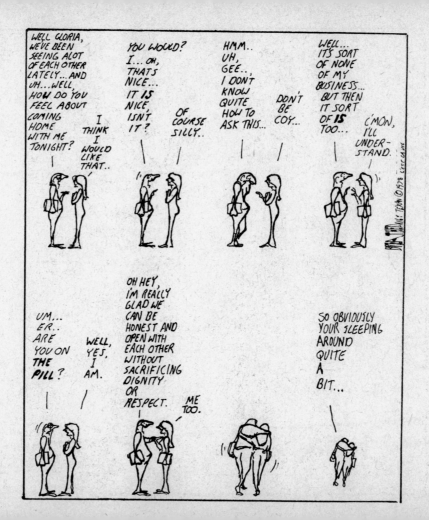

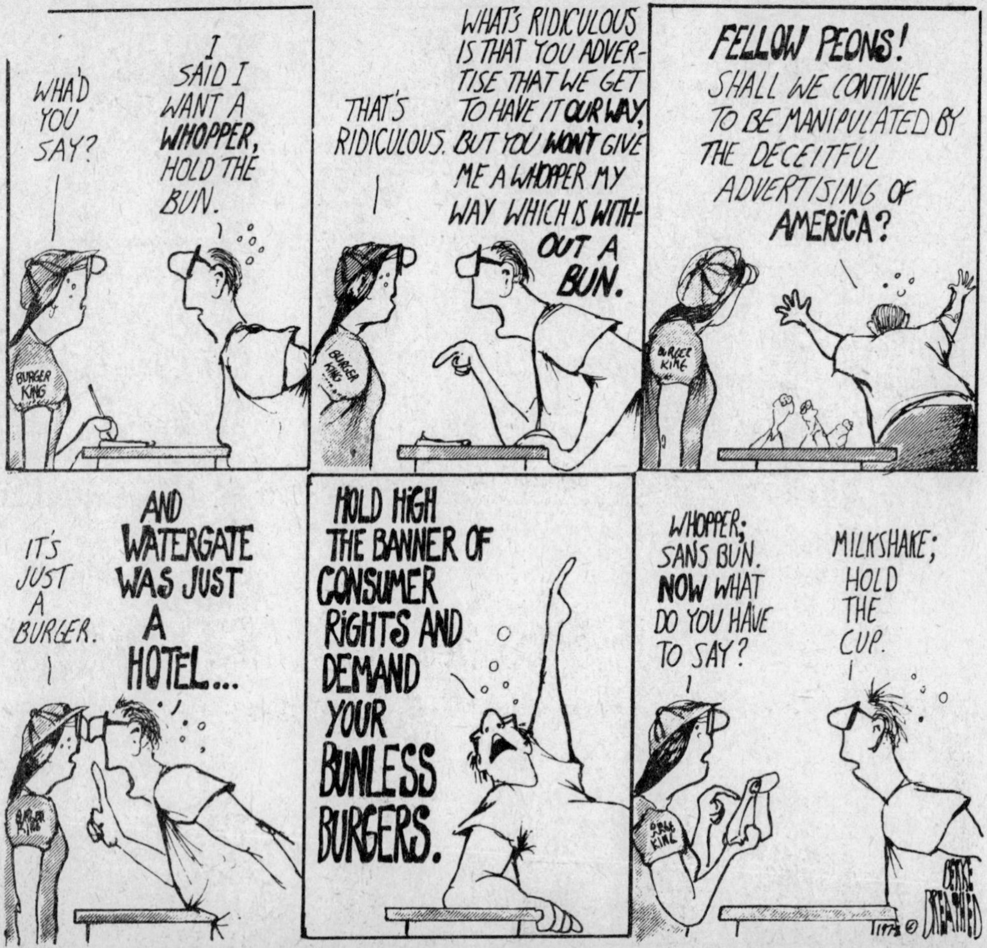
WHA'D YOU SAY?
I SAID I WANT A WHOPPER, HOLD THE BUN.
THAT'S RIDICULOUS.
WHAT'S RIDICULOUS IS THAT YOU ADVERTISE THAT WE GET TO HAVE IT OUR WAY, BUT YOU WON'T GIVE ME A WHOPPER MY WAY WHICH IS WITHOUT A BUN.
BURGER KING
FELLOW PEONS! SHALL WE CONTINUE TO BE MANIPULATED BY THE DECEITFUL ADVERTISING OF AMERICA?
IT'S JUST A BURGER.
AND WATERGATE WAS JUST A HOTEL...
HOLD HIGH THE BANNER OF CONSUMER RIGHTS AND DEMAND YOUR BUNLESS BURGERS.
WHOPPER; SANS BUN. NOW WHAT DO YOU HAVE TO SAY?
MILKSHAKE; HOLD THE CUP.
BERKE BREATHED

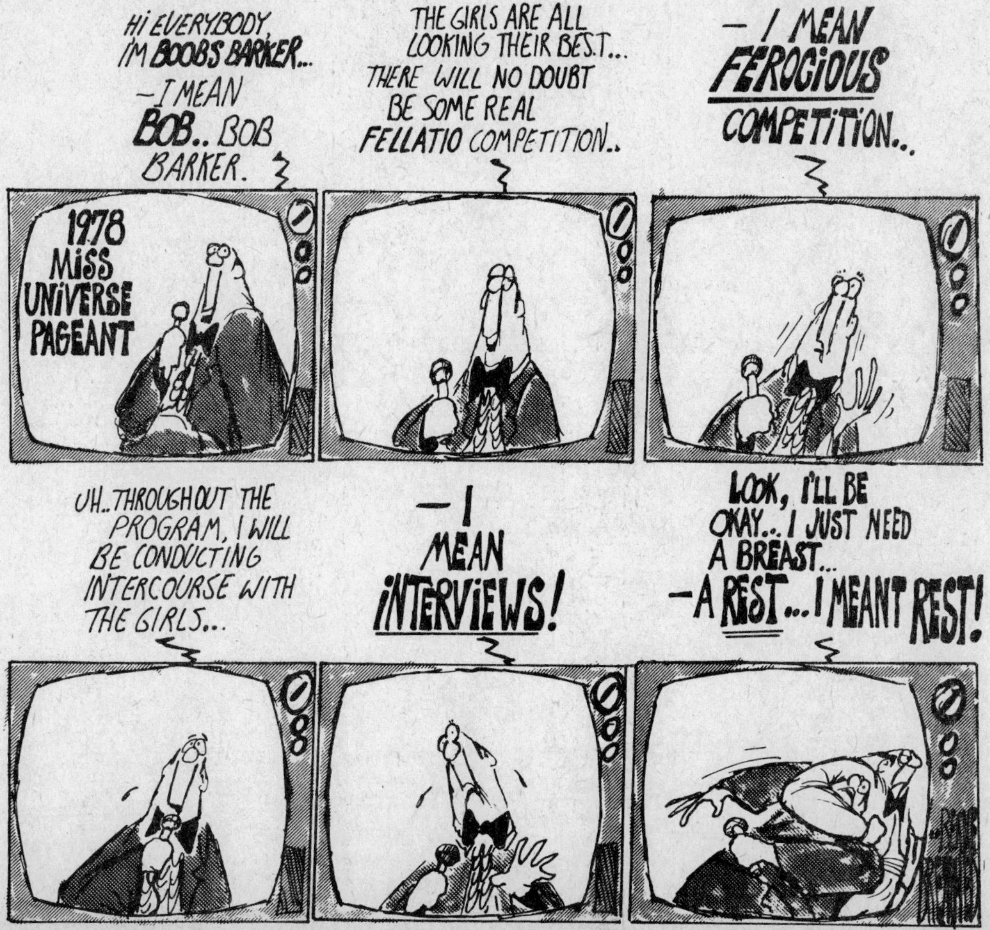
HI EVERYBODY, I'M BOOBS BARKER... —I MEAN BOB.. BOB BARKER.
1978 MISS UNIVERSE PAGEANT
THE GIRLS ARE ALL LOOKING THEIR BEST... THERE WILL NO DOUBT BE SOME REAL FELLATIO COMPETITION..
— I MEAN FEROCIOUS COMPETITION...
UH.. THROUGHOUT THE PROGRAM, I WILL BE CONDUCTING INTERCOURSE WITH THE GIRLS...
— I MEAN INTERVIEWS!
LOOK, I'LL BE OKAY... I JUST NEED A BREAST... —A REST... I MEANT REST!

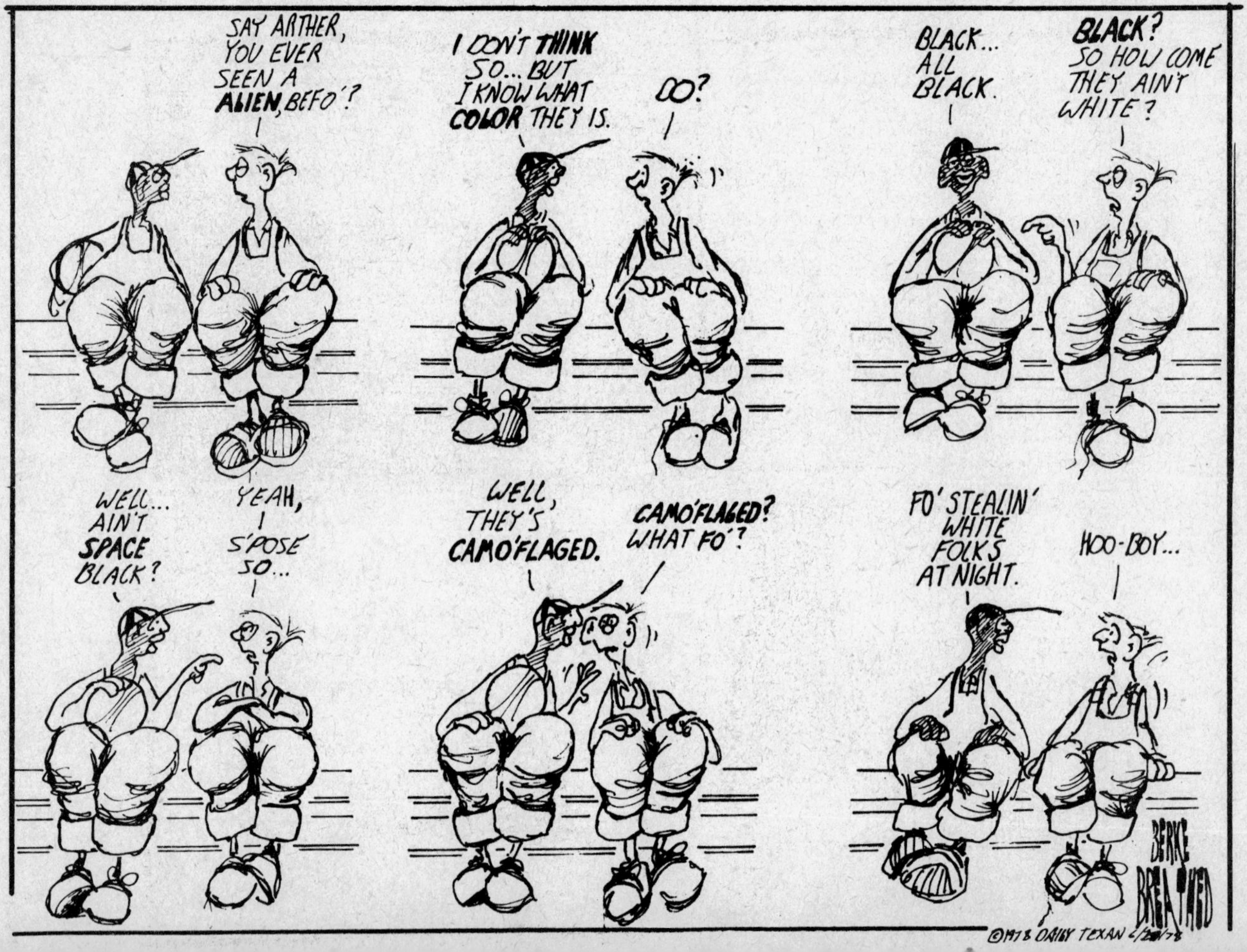
SAY ARTHER, YOU EVER SEEN A **ALIEN**, BEFO'?
I DON'T **THINK** SO... BUT I KNOW WHAT **COLOR** THEY IS.
DO?
BLACK... ALL BLACK.
BLACK? SO HOW COME THEY AIN'T WHITE?
WELL... AIN'T **SPACE** BLACK?
YEAH, I S'POSE SO...
WELL, THEY'S **CAMO'FLAGED.**
CAMO'FLAGED? WHAT FO'?
FO' STEALIN' WHITE FOLKS AT NIGHT.
HOO-BOY...
BERKE BREATHED
©1978 DAILY TEXAN

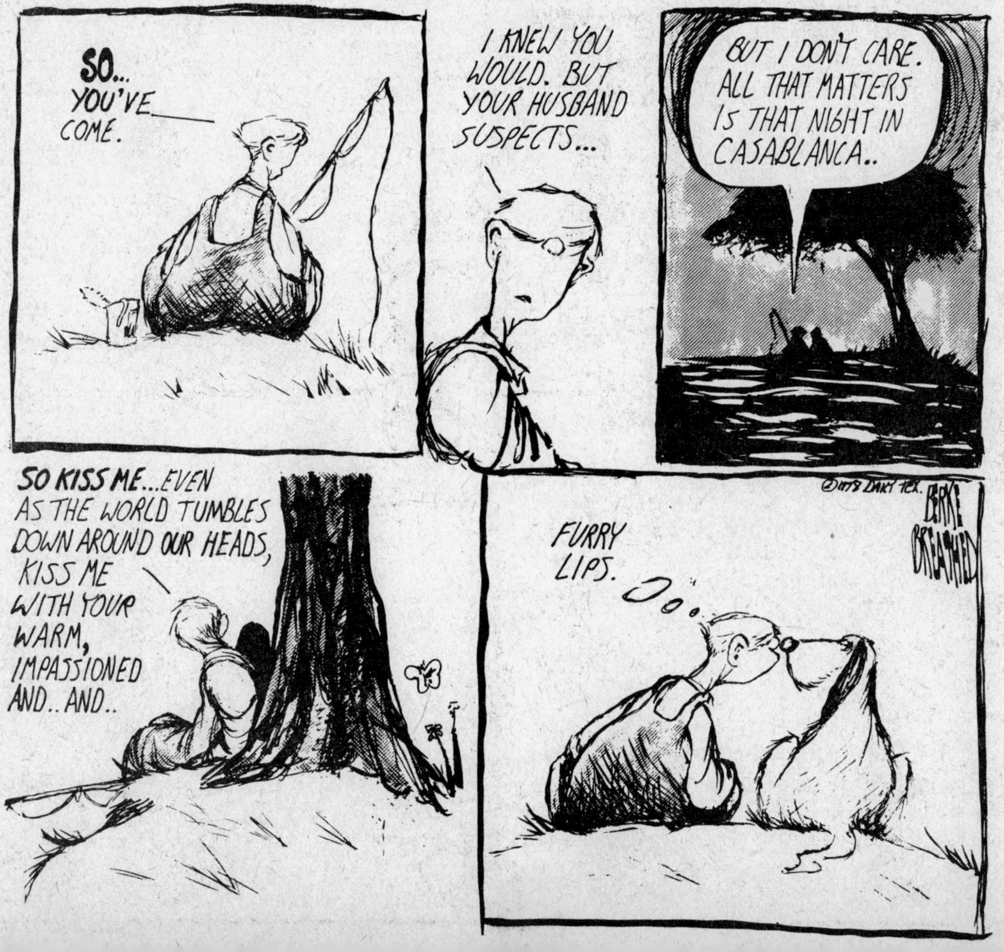
SO... YOU'VE COME.
I KNEW YOU WOULD. BUT YOUR HUSBAND SUSPECTS...
BUT I DON'T CARE. ALL THAT MATTERS IS THAT NIGHT IN CASABLANCA..
SO KISS ME...EVEN AS THE WORLD TUMBLES DOWN AROUND OUR HEADS, KISS ME WITH YOUR WARM, IMPASSIONED AND.. AND..
FURRY LIPS.

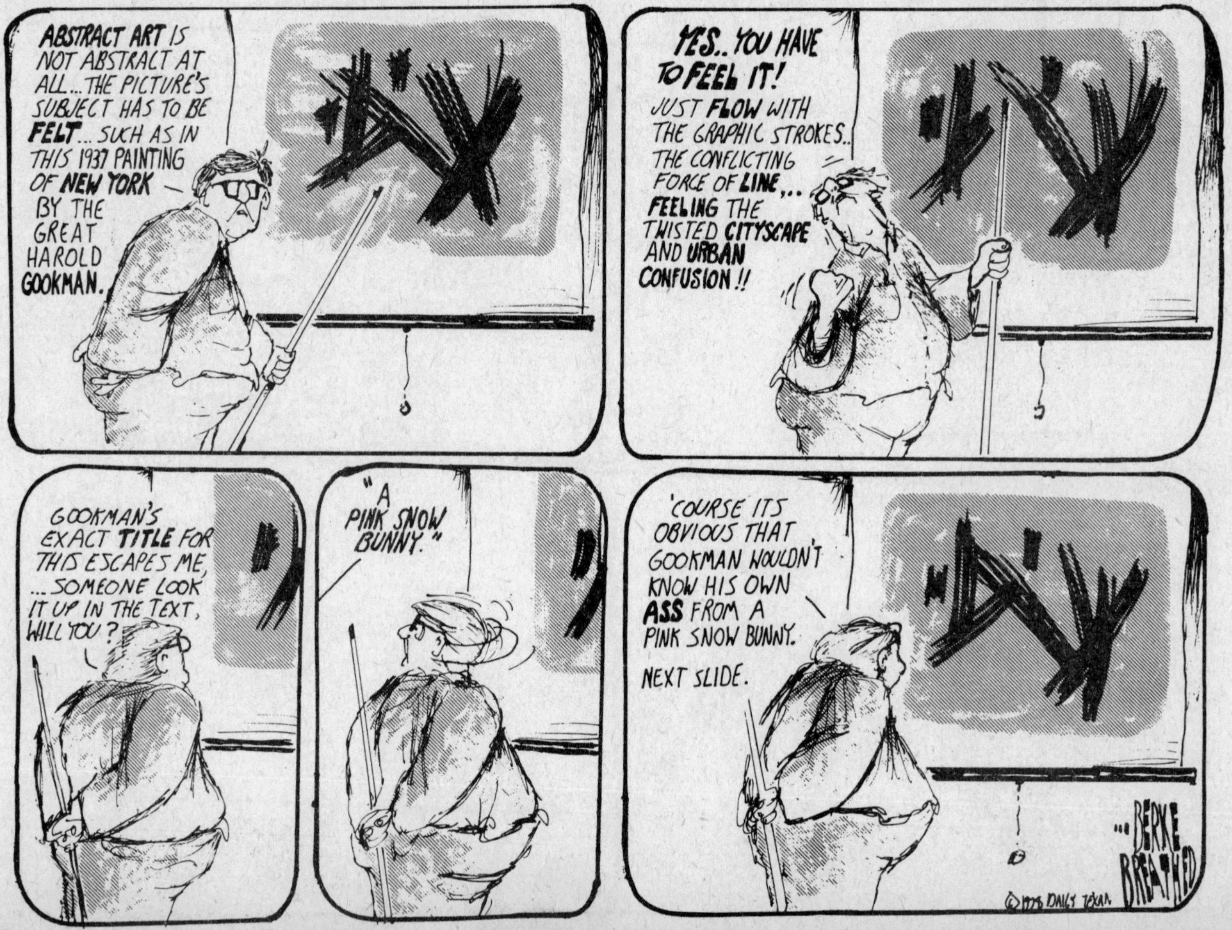
ABSTRACT ART IS NOT ABSTRACT AT ALL... THE PICTURE'S SUBJECT HAS TO BE FELT... SUCH AS IN THIS 1937 PAINTING OF NEW YORK BY THE GREAT HAROLD GOOKMAN.
YES.. YOU HAVE TO FEEL IT! JUST FLOW WITH THE GRAPHIC STROKES.. THE CONFLICTING FORCE OF LINE,.. FEELING THE TWISTED CITYSCAPE AND URBAN CONFUSION !!
GOOKMAN'S EXACT TITLE FOR THIS ESCAPES ME, ... SOMEONE LOOK IT UP IN THE TEXT, WILL YOU ?
"A PINK SNOW BUNNY."
'COURSE ITS OBVIOUS THAT GOOKMAN WOULDN'T KNOW HIS OWN ASS FROM A PINK SNOW BUNNY.
NEXT SLIDE.
...BERKE BREATHED
© 1978 DAILY TEXAN

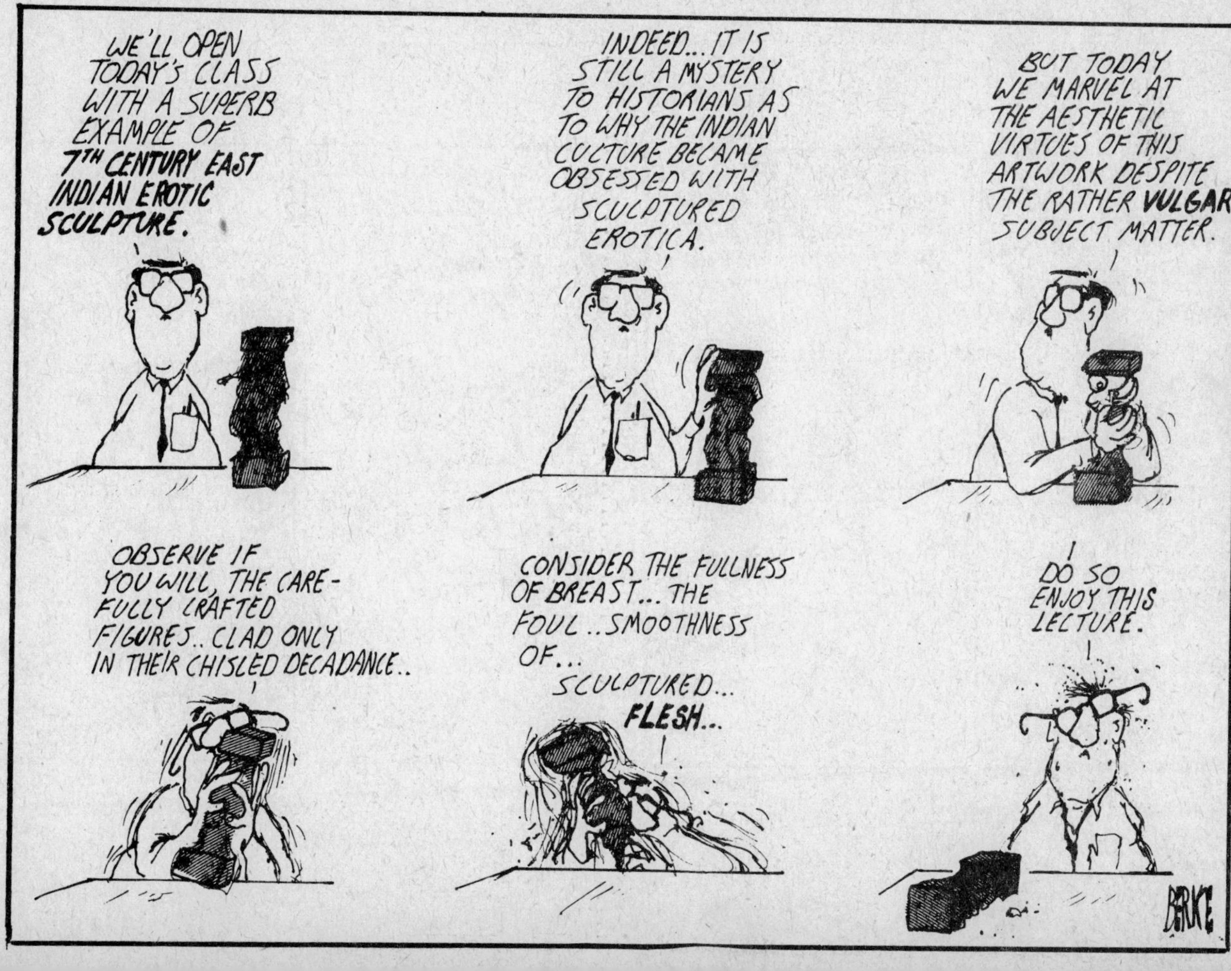
WE'LL OPEN TODAY'S CLASS WITH A SUPERB EXAMPLE OF 7TH CENTURY EAST INDIAN EROTIC SCULPTURE.
INDEED... IT IS STILL A MYSTERY TO HISTORIANS AS TO WHY THE INDIAN CULTURE BECAME OBSESSED WITH SCULPTURED EROTICA.
BUT TODAY WE MARVEL AT THE AESTHETIC VIRTUES OF THIS ARTWORK DESPITE THE RATHER VULGAR SUBJECT MATTER.
OBSERVE IF YOU WILL, THE CARE-FULLY CRAFTED FIGURES.. CLAD ONLY IN THEIR CHISLED DECADANCE..
CONSIDER THE FULLNESS OF BREAST... THE FOUL ..SMOOTHNESS OF...
SCULPTURED...
FLESH...
DO SO ENJOY THIS LECTURE.
BERKE

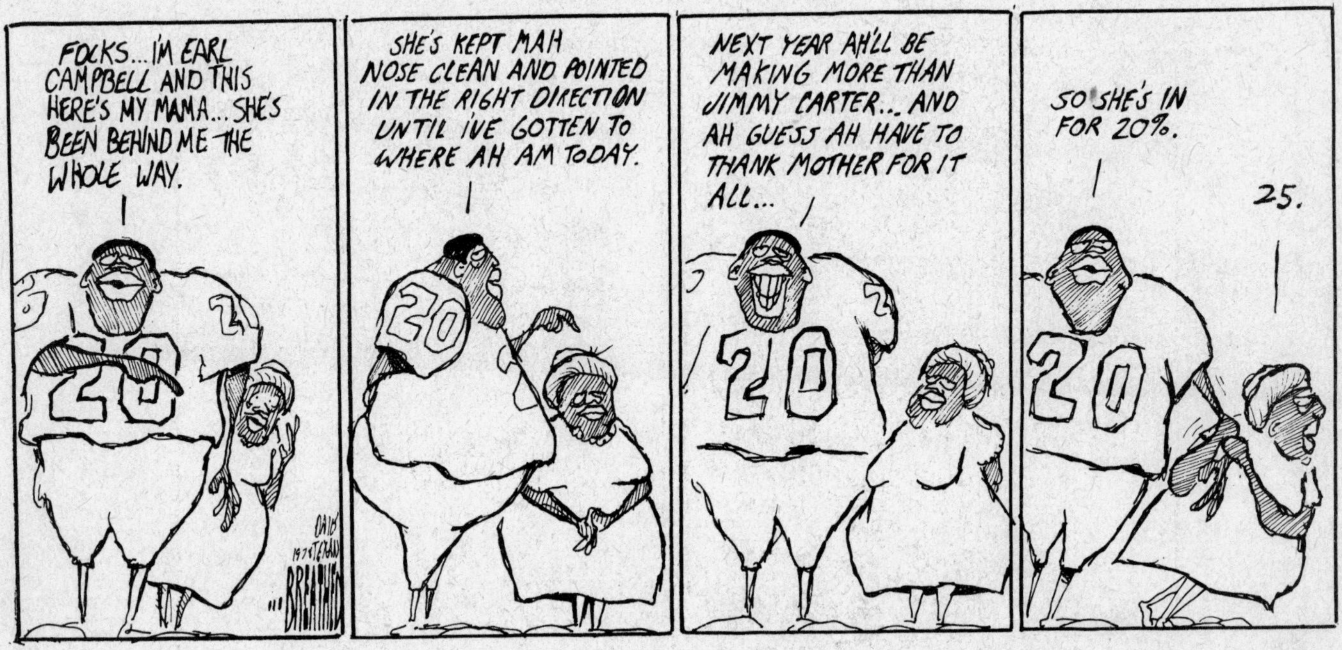
FOLKS... I'M EARL CAMPBELL AND THIS HERE'S MY MAMA... SHE'S BEEN BEHIND ME THE WHOLE WAY.
SHE'S KEPT MAH NOSE CLEAN AND POINTED IN THE RIGHT DIRECTION UNTIL I'VE GOTTEN TO WHERE AH AM TODAY.
NEXT YEAR AH'LL BE MAKING MORE THAN JIMMY CARTER... AND AH GUESS AH HAVE TO THANK MOTHER FOR IT ALL...
SO SHE'S IN FOR 20%.
25.

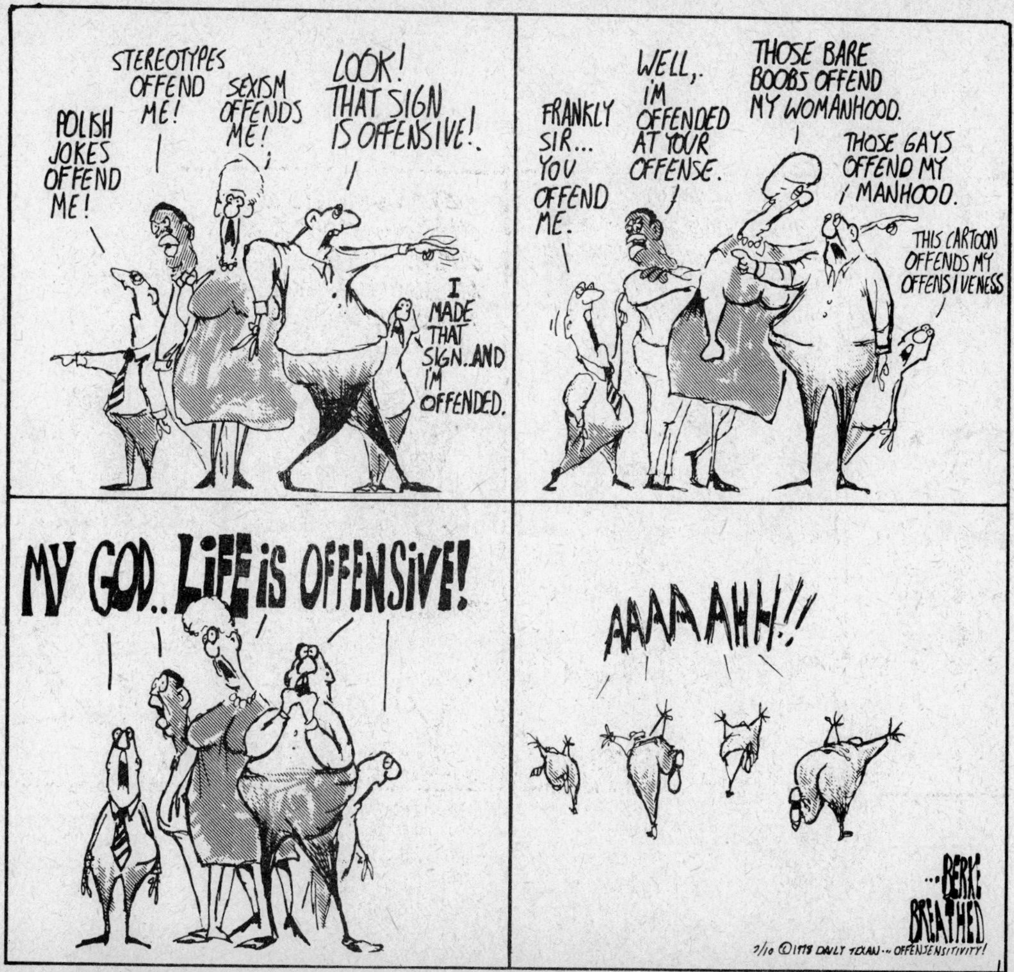

POLISH JOKES OFFEND ME!
STEREOTYPES OFFEND ME!
SEXISM OFFENDS ME!
LOOK! THAT SIGN IS OFFENSIVE!.
I MADE THAT SIGN..AND I'M OFFENDED.
FRANKLY SIR... YOU OFFEND ME.
WELL,. I'M OFFENDED AT YOUR OFFENSE.
THOSE BARE BOOBS OFFEND MY WOMANHOOD.
THOSE GAYS OFFEND MY MANHOOD.
THIS CARTOON OFFENDS MY OFFENSIVENESS
MY GOD.. LIFE IS OFFENSIVE!
AAAAAHH!!
...BERKE BREATHED
2/10 ©1978 DAILY TEXAN -- OFFENSENSITIVITY!

II

THE ACADEMIA W

ALTZ

WELL, MY FIRST DAY INSTRUCTING A UNIVERSITY COURSE... SURE IS A RELIEF NOT TO BE TEACHING 9TH GRADE MATH ANYMORE.
GAD... I DON'T THINK I COULD HAVE TAKEN ANOTHER DAY OF THOSE KIDS.
HELL.. THEY WERE SO NOISY... SO INATTENTIVE... SO... SO...
TERRIBLY, TERRIBLY YOUNG.

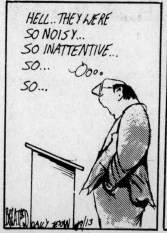

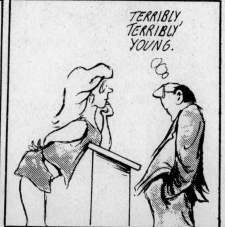

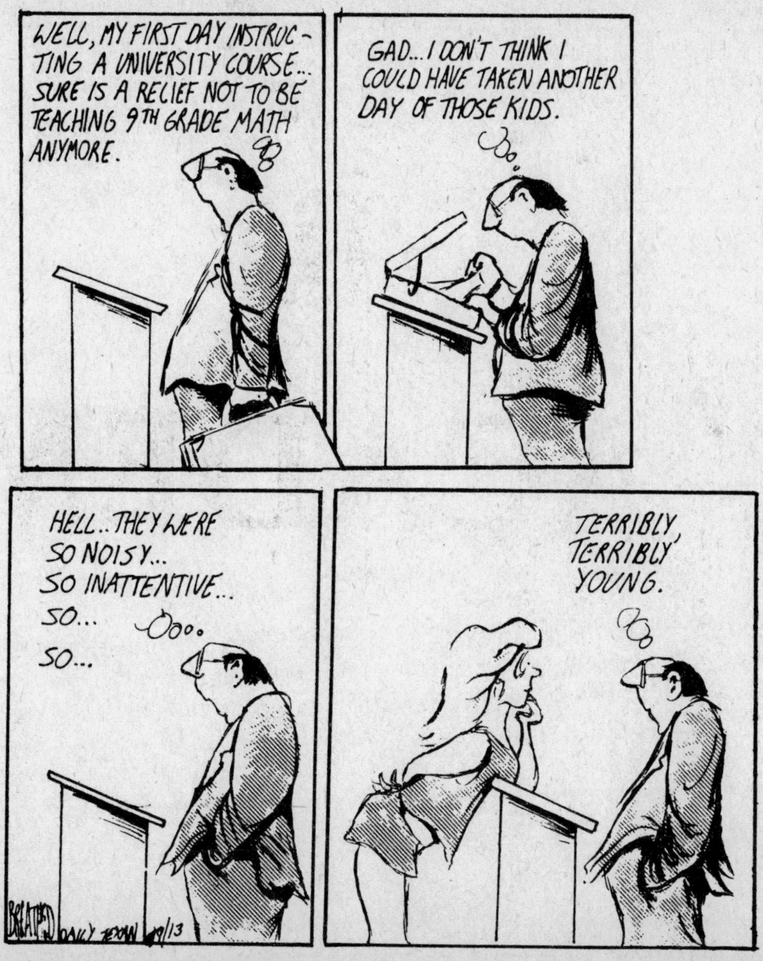

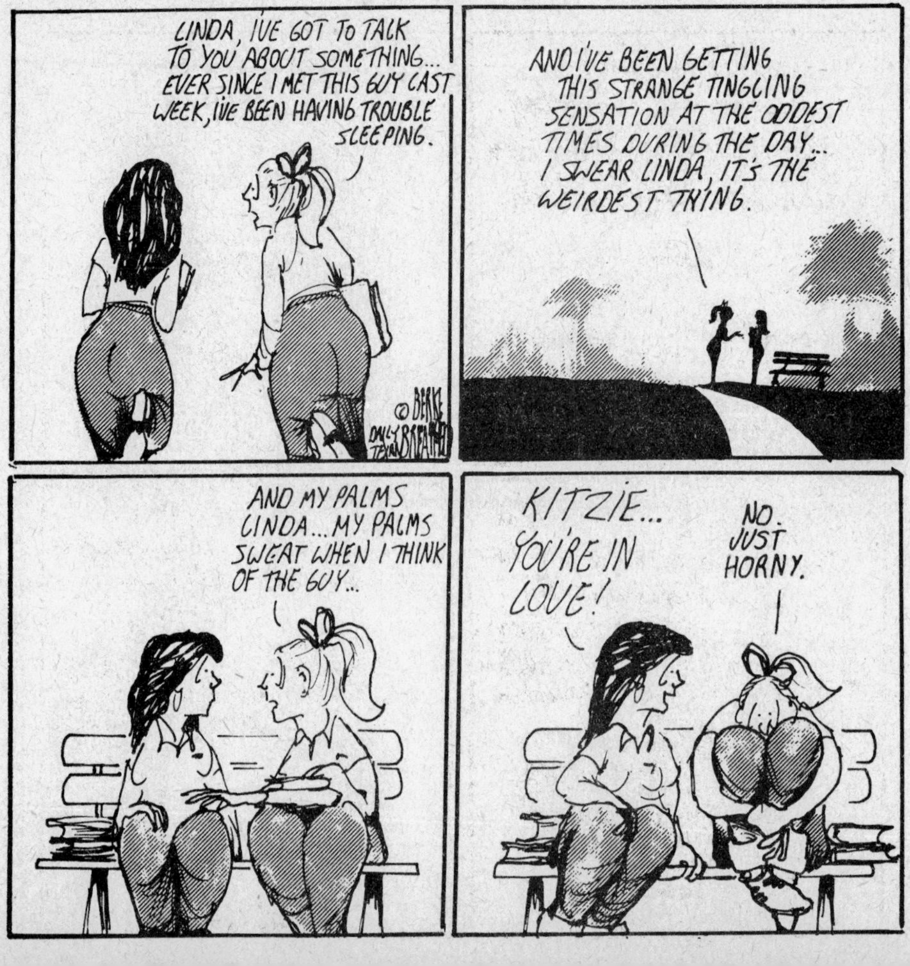

LINDA, I'VE GOT TO TALK TO YOU ABOUT SOMETHING... EVER SINCE I MET THIS GUY LAST WEEK, I'VE BEEN HAVING TROUBLE SLEEPING.
© BERKE BREATHED
AND I'VE BEEN GETTING THIS STRANGE TINGLING SENSATION AT THE ODDEST TIMES DURING THE DAY... I SWEAR LINDA, IT'S THE WEIRDEST THING.
AND MY PALMS LINDA... MY PALMS SWEAT WHEN I THINK OF THE GUY...
KITZIE... YOU'RE IN LOVE!
NO. JUST HORNY.

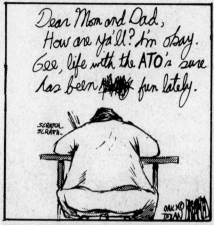

Dear Mom and Dad,
How are ya'll? I'm okay.
Gee, life with the ATO's sure
has been fun lately.
SCRATCH.. SCRATCH..
DAILY© TEXAN
...lots of excitement,
lots of exercise...
its just like you say Mom;
we're just a bunch of
wild and crazy guys.
SCRATCH SCRATCH
9/12
You'll be glad to hear that
ATO community interaction has
been at its highest recently...
fact; seems as if just about every-
body is talking about our close relations
with others in the neighborhood.
SCRATCH SCRATCH SCRATCH
Well, I guess thats all...
I think they're calling me for
dinner. Say hello to Sis.
Your Son,
Ralph
Travis County Jail
Austin, Texas
78706
SCRATCH SCRATCH

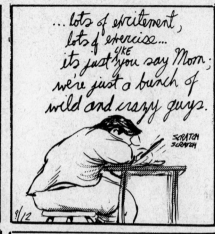

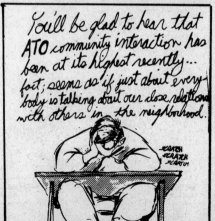

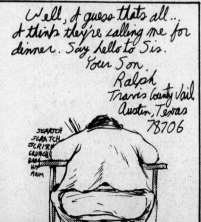

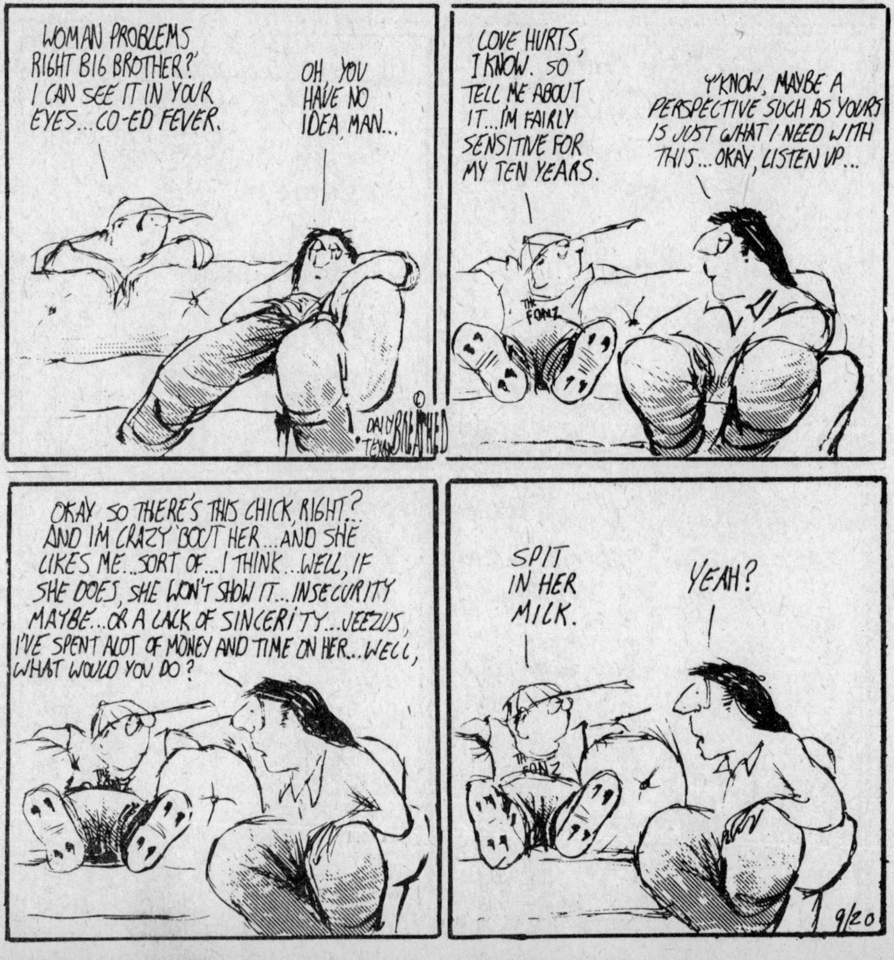
WOMAN PROBLEMS RIGHT BIG BROTHER? I CAN SEE IT IN YOUR EYES...CO-ED FEVER.
OH YOU HAVE NO IDEA, MAN...
© DAILY TEXAN BREATHED
LOVE HURTS, I KNOW. SO TELL ME ABOUT IT...I'M FAIRLY SENSITIVE FOR MY TEN YEARS.
Y'KNOW, MAYBE A PERSPECTIVE SUCH AS YOURS IS JUST WHAT I NEED WITH THIS...OKAY, LISTEN UP...
THE FONZ
OKAY SO THERE'S THIS CHICK, RIGHT?... AND I'M CRAZY 'BOUT HER...AND SHE LIKES ME...SORT OF...I THINK...WELL, IF SHE DOES, SHE WON'T SHOW IT...INSECURITY MAYBE...OR A LACK OF SINCERITY...JEEZUS, I'VE SPENT ALOT OF MONEY AND TIME ON HER...WELL, WHAT WOULD YOU DO?
SPIT IN HER MILK.
YEAH?
THE FONZ
9/20

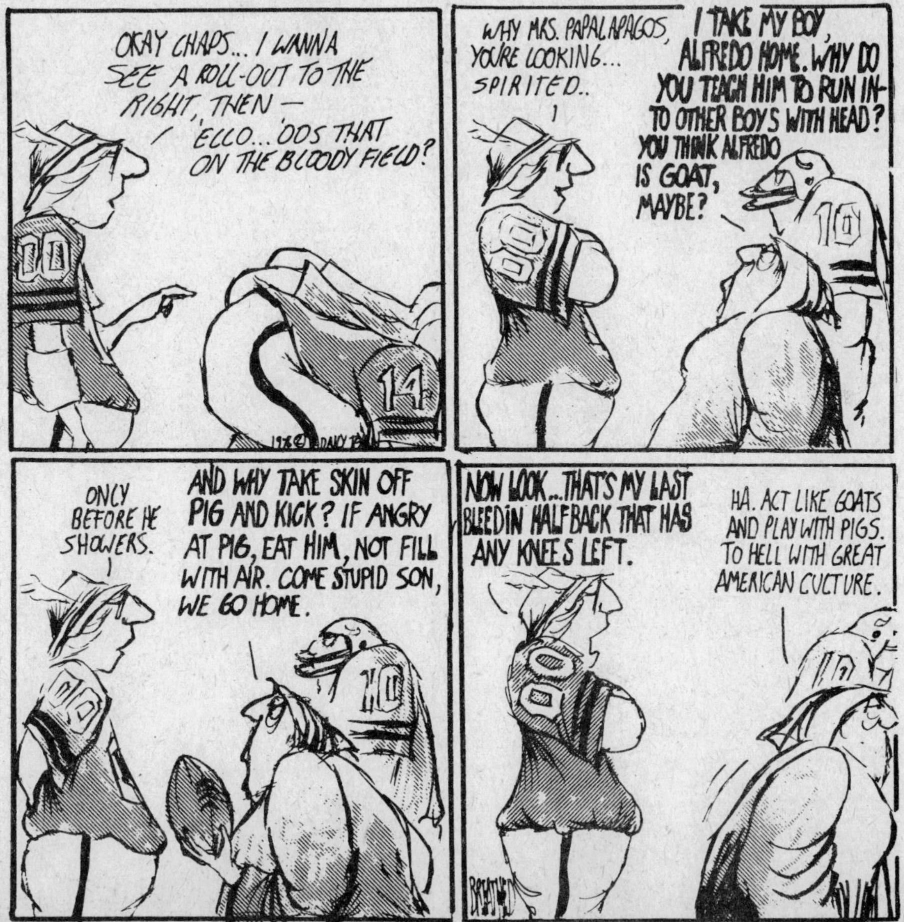
OKAY CHAPS... I WANNA SEE A ROLL-OUT TO THE RIGHT, THEN —
'ELLO... 'OOS THAT ON THE BLOODY FIELD?
WHY MRS. PAPALAPAGOS, YOU'RE LOOKING... SPIRITED..
I TAKE MY BOY, ALFREDO HOME. WHY DO YOU TEACH HIM TO RUN INTO OTHER BOYS WITH HEAD? YOU THINK ALFREDO IS GOAT, MAYBE?
ONLY BEFORE HE SHOWERS.
AND WHY TAKE SKIN OFF PIG AND KICK? IF ANGRY AT PIG, EAT HIM, NOT FILL WITH AIR. COME STUPID SON, WE GO HOME.
NOW LOOK...THAT'S MY LAST BLEEDIN HALFBACK THAT HAS ANY KNEES LEFT.
HA. ACT LIKE GOATS AND PLAY WITH PIGS. TO HELL WITH GREAT AMERICAN CULTURE.

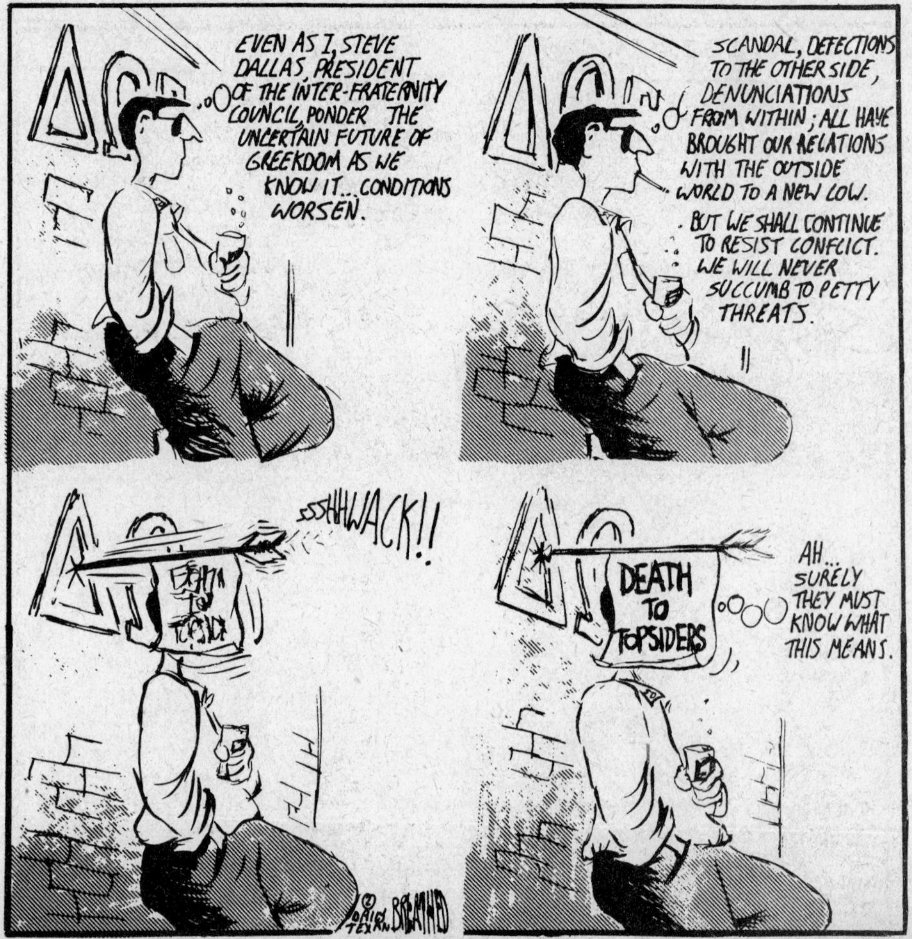
EVEN AS I, STEVE DALLAS, PRESIDENT OF THE INTER-FRATERNITY COUNCIL, PONDER THE UNCERTAIN FUTURE OF GREEKDOM AS WE KNOW IT... CONDITIONS WORSEN.
SCANDAL, DEFECTIONS TO THE OTHER SIDE, DENUNCIATIONS FROM WITHIN; ALL HAVE BROUGHT OUR RELATIONS WITH THE OUTSIDE WORLD TO A NEW LOW.
BUT WE SHALL CONTINUE TO RESIST CONFLICT. WE WILL NEVER SUCCUMB TO PETTY THREATS.
SSSHHWACK!!
DEATH TO TOPSIDERS
AH... SURELY THEY MUST KNOW WHAT THIS MEANS.
© DAILY TEXAN BREATHED

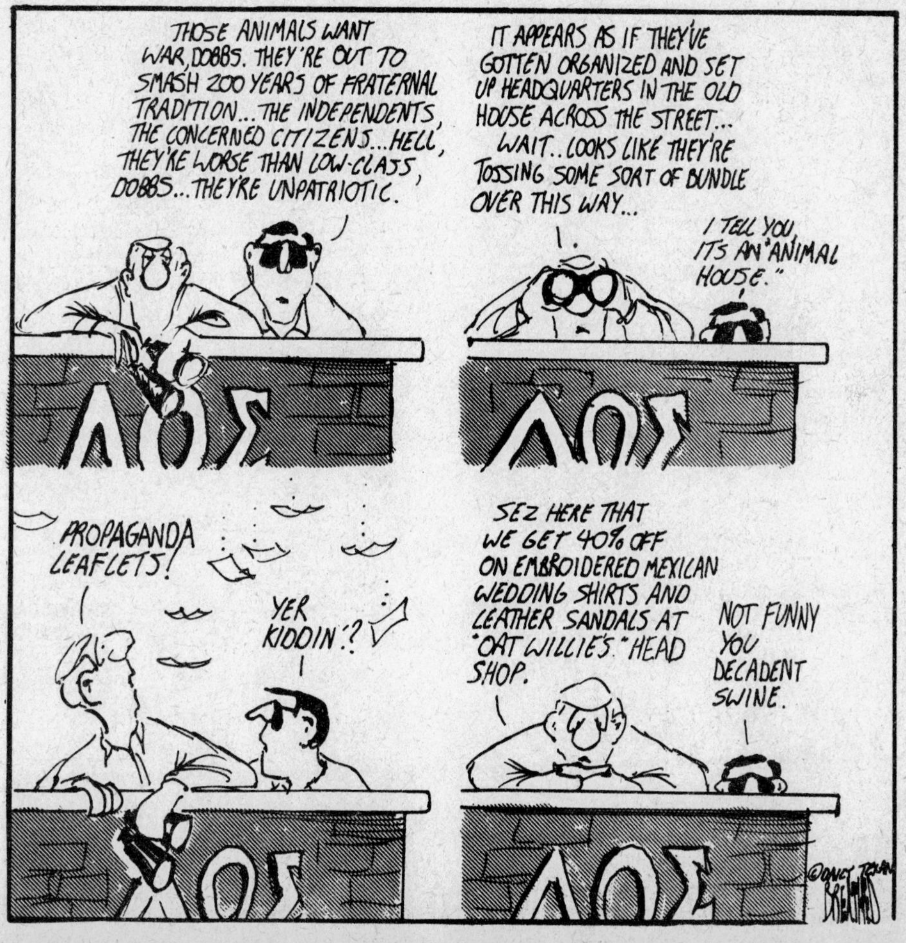
THOSE ANIMALS WANT WAR, DOBBS. THEY'RE OUT TO SMASH 200 YEARS OF FRATERNAL TRADITION... THE INDEPENDENTS, THE CONCERNED CITIZENS... HELL, THEY'RE WORSE THAN LOW-CLASS, DOBBS... THEY'RE UNPATRIOTIC.
IT APPEARS AS IF THEY'VE GOTTEN ORGANIZED AND SET UP HEADQUARTERS IN THE OLD HOUSE ACROSS THE STREET... WAIT.. LOOKS LIKE THEY'RE TOSSING SOME SORT OF BUNDLE OVER THIS WAY...
I TELL YOU, ITS AN "ANIMAL HOUSE."
ΛΩΣ
PROPAGANDA LEAFLETS!
YER KIDDIN'?
SEZ HERE THAT WE GET 40% OFF ON EMBROIDERED MEXICAN WEDDING SHIRTS AND LEATHER SANDALS AT "OAT WILLIE'S" HEAD SHOP.
NOT FUNNY YOU DECADENT SWINE.
©DAILY TEXAN
BREATHED

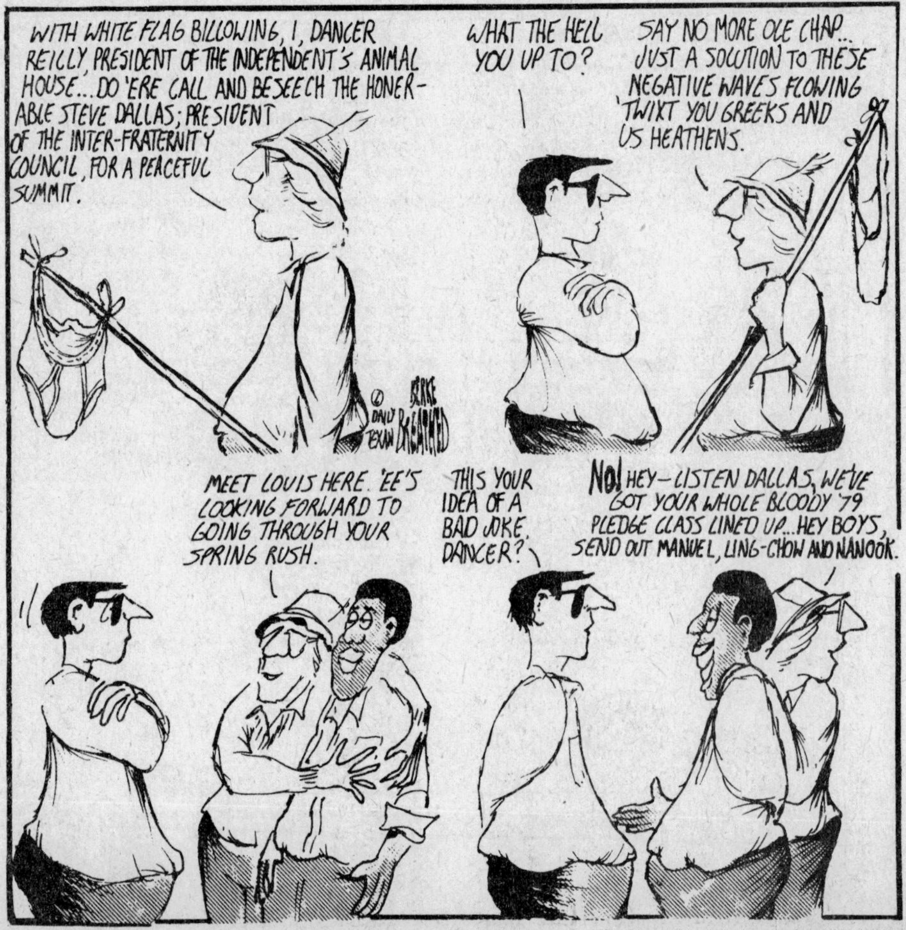
WITH WHITE FLAG BILLOWING, I, DANCER REILLY, PRESIDENT OF THE INDEPENDENT'S ANIMAL HOUSE... DO 'ERE CALL AND BESEECH THE HONER-ABLE STEVE DALLAS; PRESIDENT OF THE INTER-FRATERNITY COUNCIL, FOR A PEACEFUL SUMMIT.
WHAT THE HELL YOU UP TO?
SAY NO MORE OLE CHAP... JUST A SOLUTION TO THESE NEGATIVE WAVES FLOWING 'TWIXT YOU GREEKS AND US HEATHENS.
MEET LOUIS HERE. 'EE'S LOOKING FORWARD TO GOING THROUGH YOUR SPRING RUSH.
THIS YOUR IDEA OF A BAD JOKE, DANCER?
NO! HEY—LISTEN DALLAS, WE'VE GOT YOUR WHOLE BLOODY '79 PLEDGE CLASS LINED UP... HEY BOYS, SEND OUT MANUEL, LING-CHOW AND NANOOK.

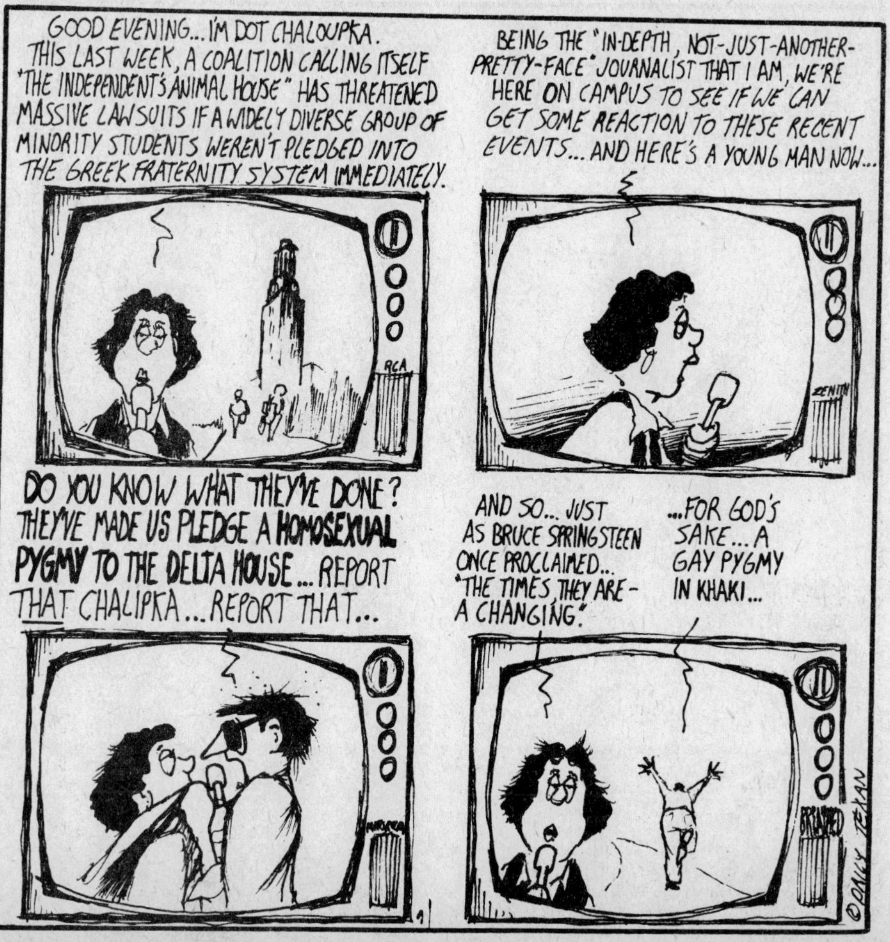
GOOD EVENING... I'M DOT CHALOUPKA.
THIS LAST WEEK, A COALITION CALLING ITSELF "THE INDEPENDENT'S ANIMAL HOUSE" HAS THREATENED MASSIVE LAWSUITS IF A WIDELY DIVERSE GROUP OF MINORITY STUDENTS WEREN'T PLEDGED INTO THE GREEK FRATERNITY SYSTEM IMMEDIATELY.
RCA
BEING THE "IN-DEPTH, NOT-JUST-ANOTHER-PRETTY-FACE" JOURNALIST THAT I AM, WE'RE HERE ON CAMPUS TO SEE IF WE CAN GET SOME REACTION TO THESE RECENT EVENTS... AND HERE'S A YOUNG MAN NOW...
ZENITH
DO YOU KNOW WHAT THEY'VE DONE? THEY'VE MADE US PLEDGE A HOMOSEXUAL PYGMY TO THE DELTA HOUSE... REPORT THAT CHALIPKA... REPORT THAT...
AND SO... JUST AS BRUCE SPRINGSTEEN ONCE PROCLAIMED... "THE TIMES, THEY ARE-A CHANGING."
...FOR GOD'S SAKE... A GAY PYGMY IN KHAKI...
©DAILY TEXAN

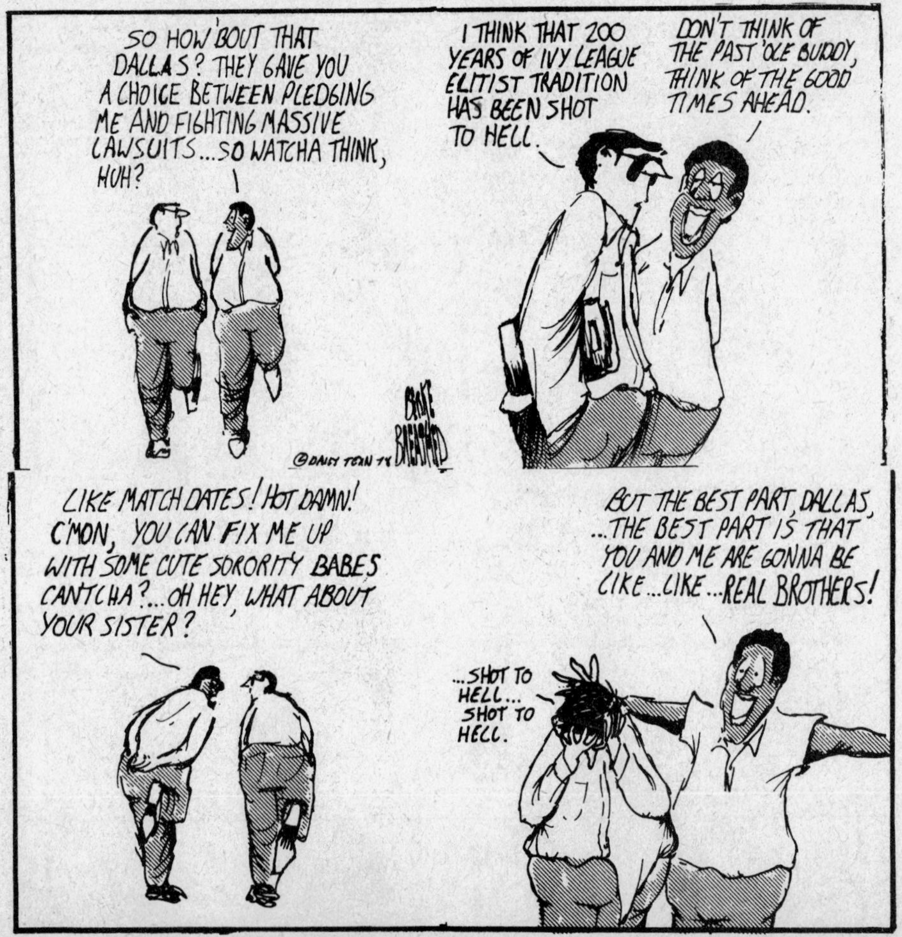
SO HOW 'BOUT THAT DALLAS? THEY GAVE YOU A CHOICE BETWEEN PLEDGING ME AND FIGHTING MASSIVE LAWSUITS...SO WATCHA THINK, HUH?
I THINK THAT 200 YEARS OF IVY LEAGUE ELITIST TRADITION HAS BEEN SHOT TO HELL.
DON'T THINK OF THE PAST 'OLE BUDDY, THINK OF THE GOOD TIMES AHEAD.
LIKE MATCH DATES! HOT DAMN! C'MON, YOU CAN FIX ME UP WITH SOME CUTE SORORITY BABES CANTCHA?...OH HEY, WHAT ABOUT YOUR SISTER?
BUT THE BEST PART, DALLAS, ...THE BEST PART IS THAT YOU AND ME ARE GONNA BE LIKE...LIKE...REAL BROTHERS!
...SHOT TO HELL... SHOT TO HELL.
BLOOM BREATHED

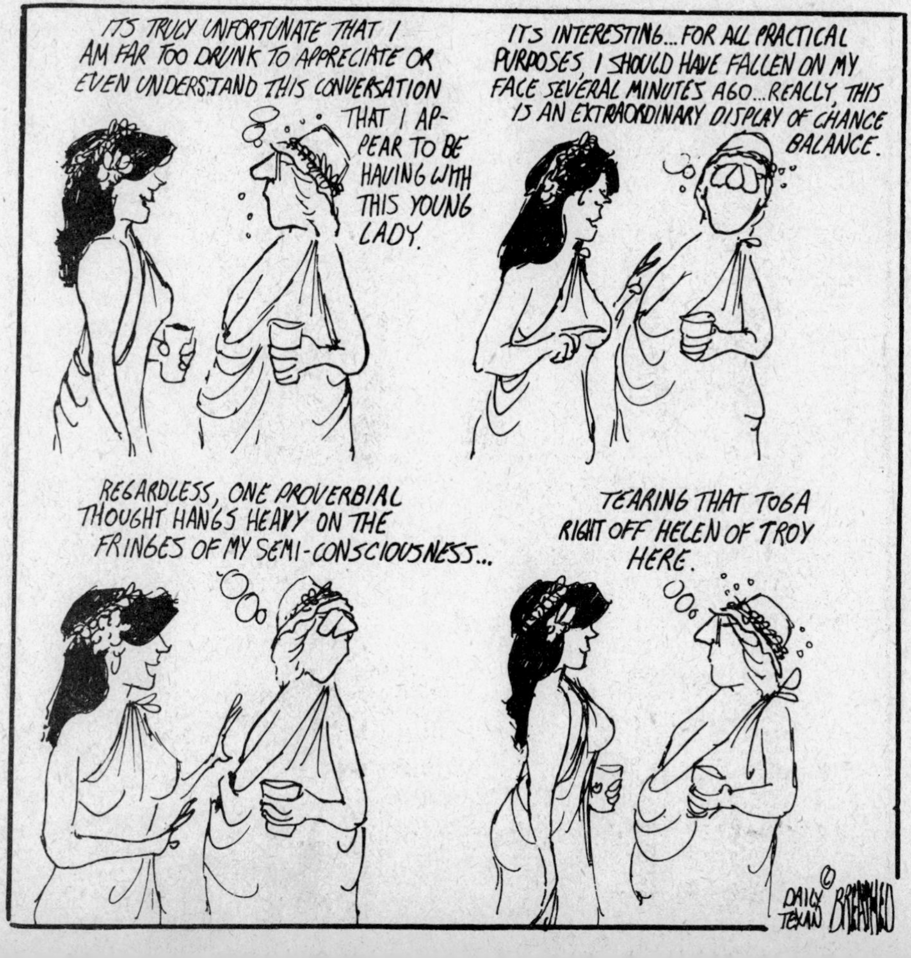
ITS TRULY UNFORTUNATE THAT I AM FAR TOO DRUNK TO APPRECIATE OR EVEN UNDERSTAND THIS CONVERSATION THAT I AP-PEAR TO BE HAVING WITH THIS YOUNG LADY.
ITS INTERESTING... FOR ALL PRACTICAL PURPOSES, I SHOULD HAVE FALLEN ON MY FACE SEVERAL MINUTES AGO... REALLY, THIS IS AN EXTRAORDINARY DISPLAY OF CHANCE BALANCE.
REGARDLESS, ONE PROVERBIAL THOUGHT HANGS HEAVY ON THE FRINGES OF MY SEMI-CONSCIOUSNESS...
TEARING THAT TOGA RIGHT OFF HELEN OF TROY HERE.
© DAILY TEXAN

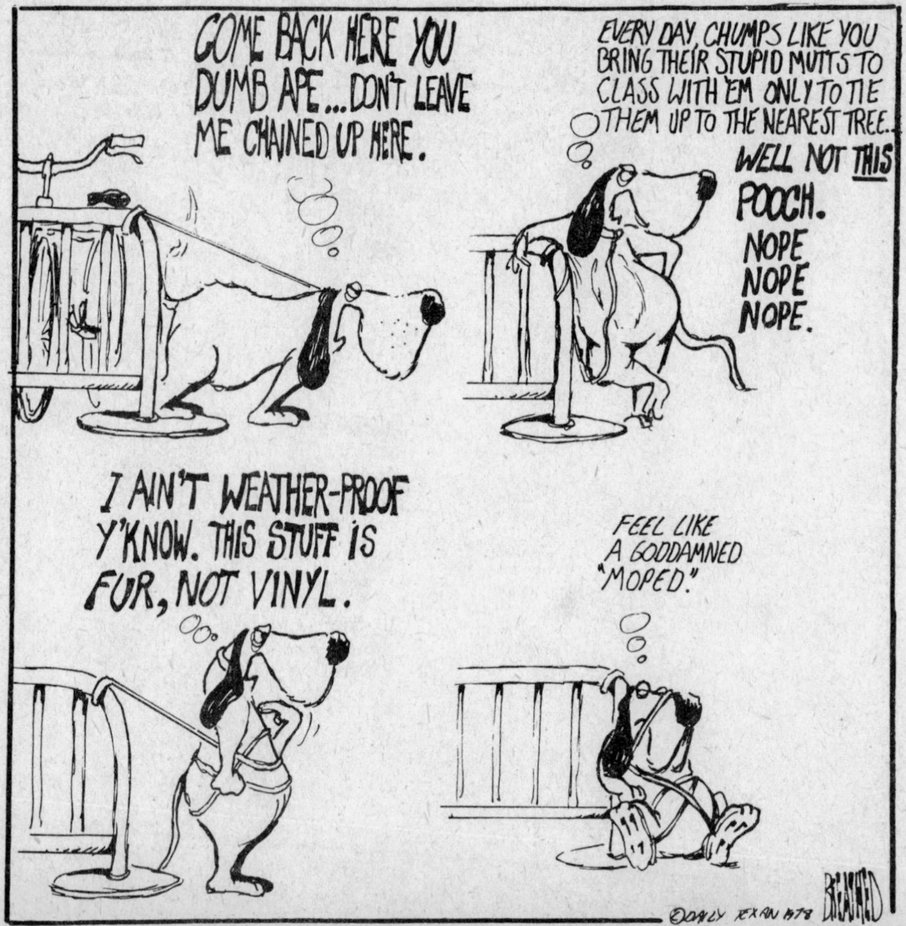
COME BACK HERE YOU DUMB APE...DON'T LEAVE ME CHAINED UP HERE.
EVERY DAY, CHUMPS LIKE YOU BRING THEIR STUPID MUTTS TO CLASS WITH 'EM ONLY TO TIE THEM UP TO THE NEAREST TREE..
WELL NOT THIS POOCH.
NOPE NOPE NOPE.
I AIN'T WEATHER-PROOF Y'KNOW. THIS STUFF IS FUR, NOT VINYL.
FEEL LIKE A GODDAMNED "MOPED."
©DAILY TEXAN 1978
BREATHED

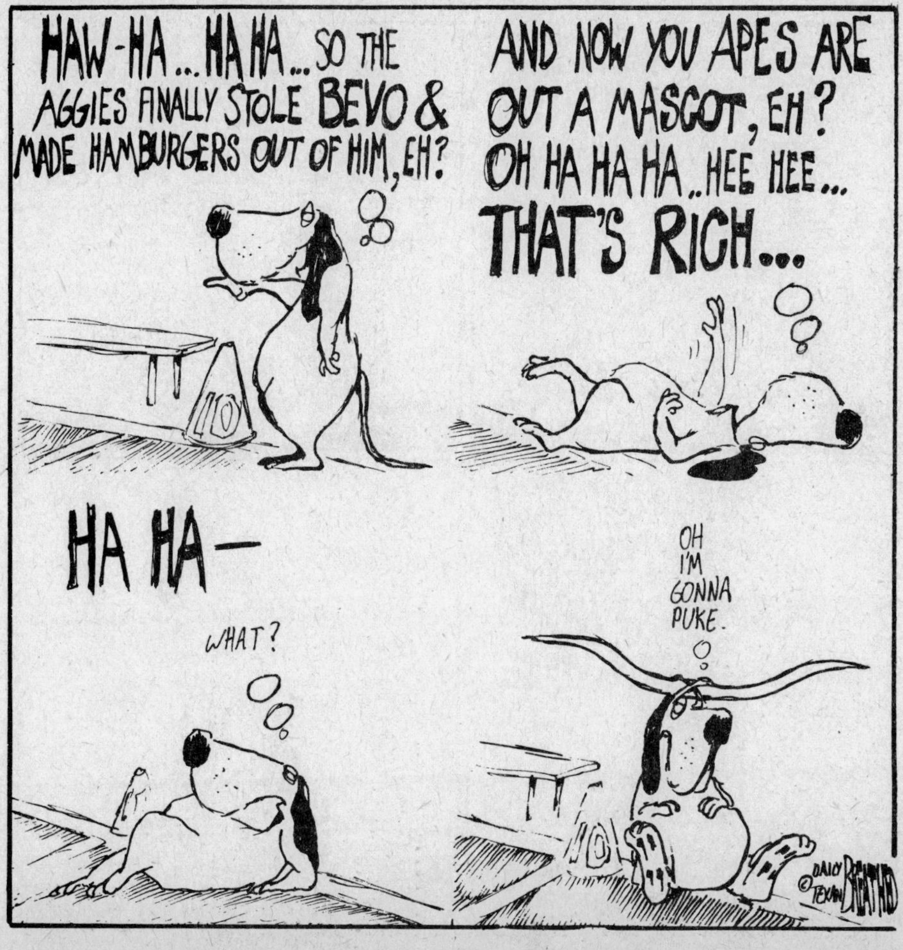
HAW-HA... HA HA... SO THE AGGIES FINALLY STOLE BEVO & MADE HAMBURGERS OUT OF HIM, EH?
AND NOW YOU APES ARE OUT A MASCOT, EH? OH HA HA HA.. HEE HEE... THAT'S RICH...
HA HA—
WHAT?
OH I'M GONNA PUKE.
© DAILY TEXAN BREATHED

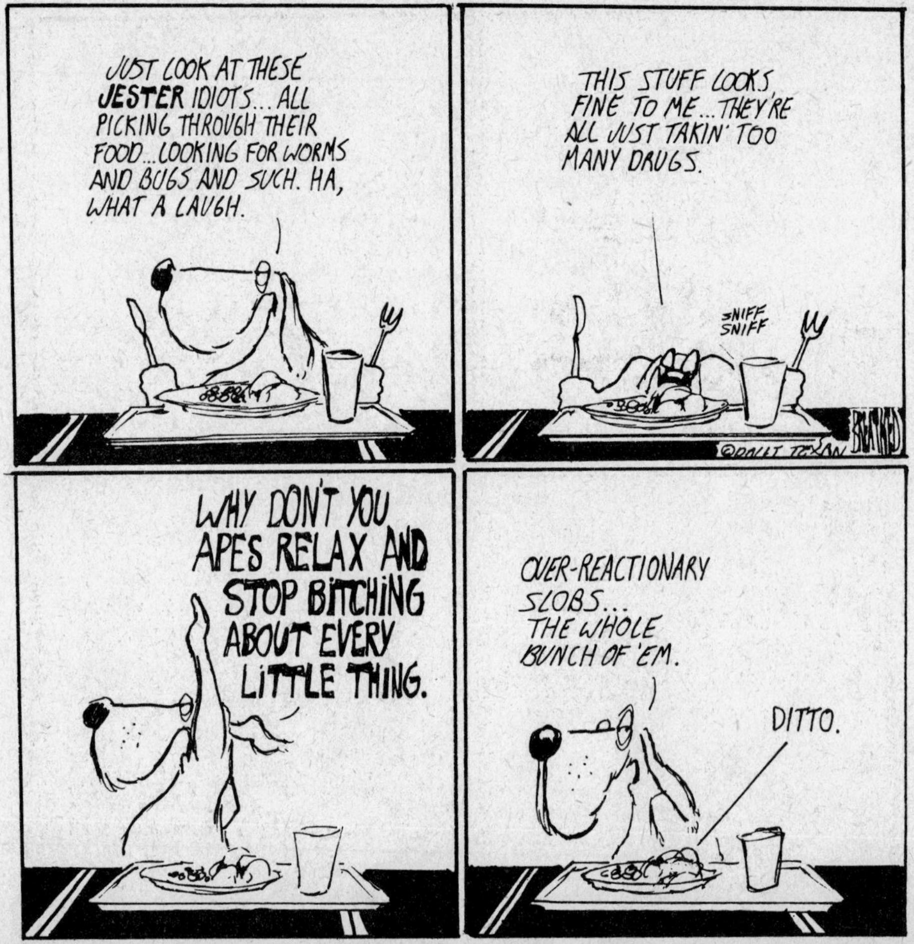
JUST LOOK AT THESE **JESTER** IDIOTS... ALL PICKING THROUGH THEIR FOOD...LOOKING FOR WORMS AND BUGS AND SUCH. HA, WHAT A LAUGH.
THIS STUFF LOOKS FINE TO ME...THEY'RE ALL JUST TAKIN' TOO MANY DRUGS.
SNIFF SNIFF
©DAILY TEXAN
BREATHED
WHY DON'T YOU APES RELAX AND STOP BITCHING ABOUT EVERY LITTLE THING.
OVER-REACTIONARY SLOBS... THE WHOLE BUNCH OF 'EM.
DITTO.

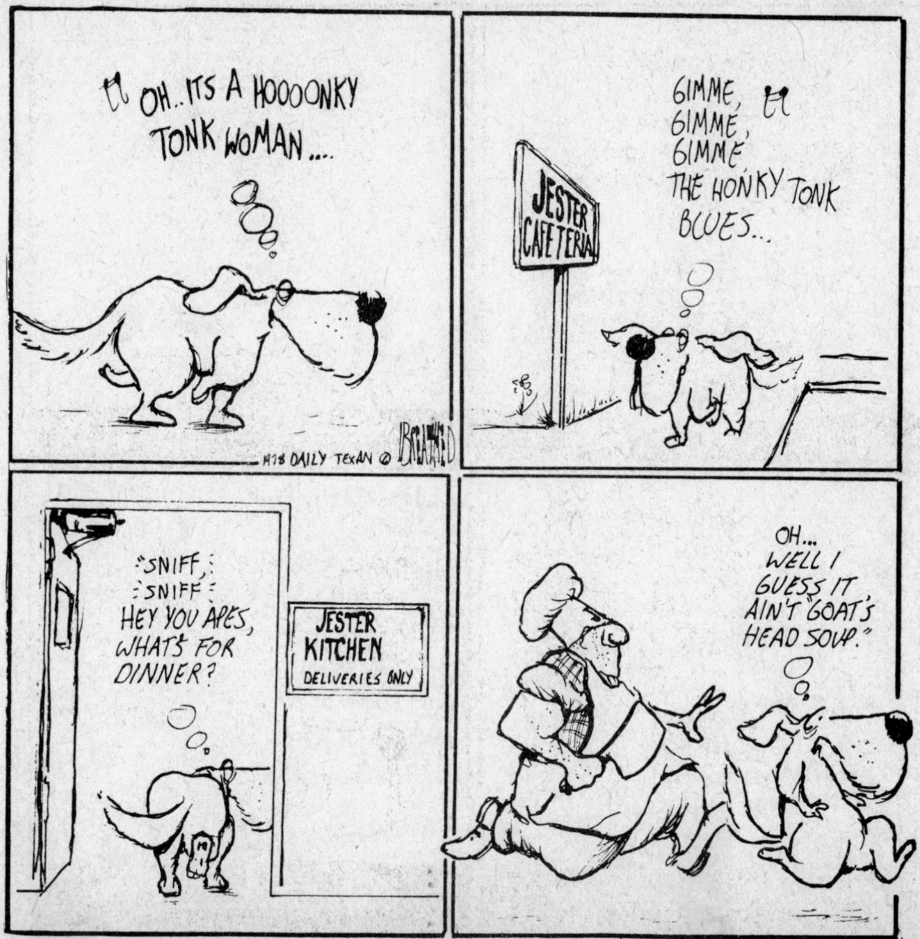
OH..ITS A HOOOONKY TONK WOMAN....
1978 DAILY TEXAN ©
GIMME, GIMME, GIMME THE HONKY TONK BLUES...
JESTER CAFETERIA
SNIFF, SNIFF
HEY YOU APES, WHAT'S FOR DINNER?
JESTER KITCHEN
DELIVERIES ONLY
OH... WELL I GUESS IT AIN'T "GOAT'S HEAD SOUP."

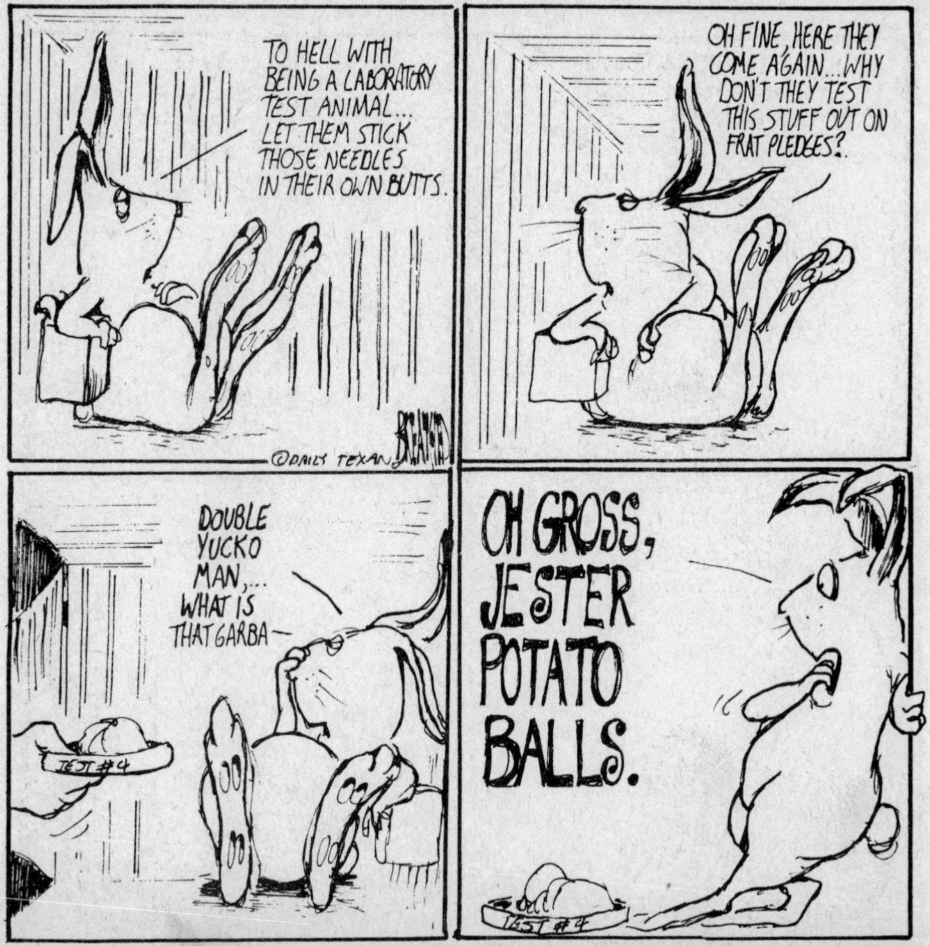
TO HELL WITH BEING A LABORATORY TEST ANIMAL... LET THEM STICK THOSE NEEDLES IN THEIR OWN BUTTS.
©DAILY TEXAN
OH FINE, HERE THEY COME AGAIN... WHY DON'T THEY TEST THIS STUFF OUT ON FRAT PLEDGES?
DOUBLE YUCKO MAN,... WHAT IS THAT GARBA—
TEST #4
OH GROSS, JESTER POTATO BALLS.
TEST #4

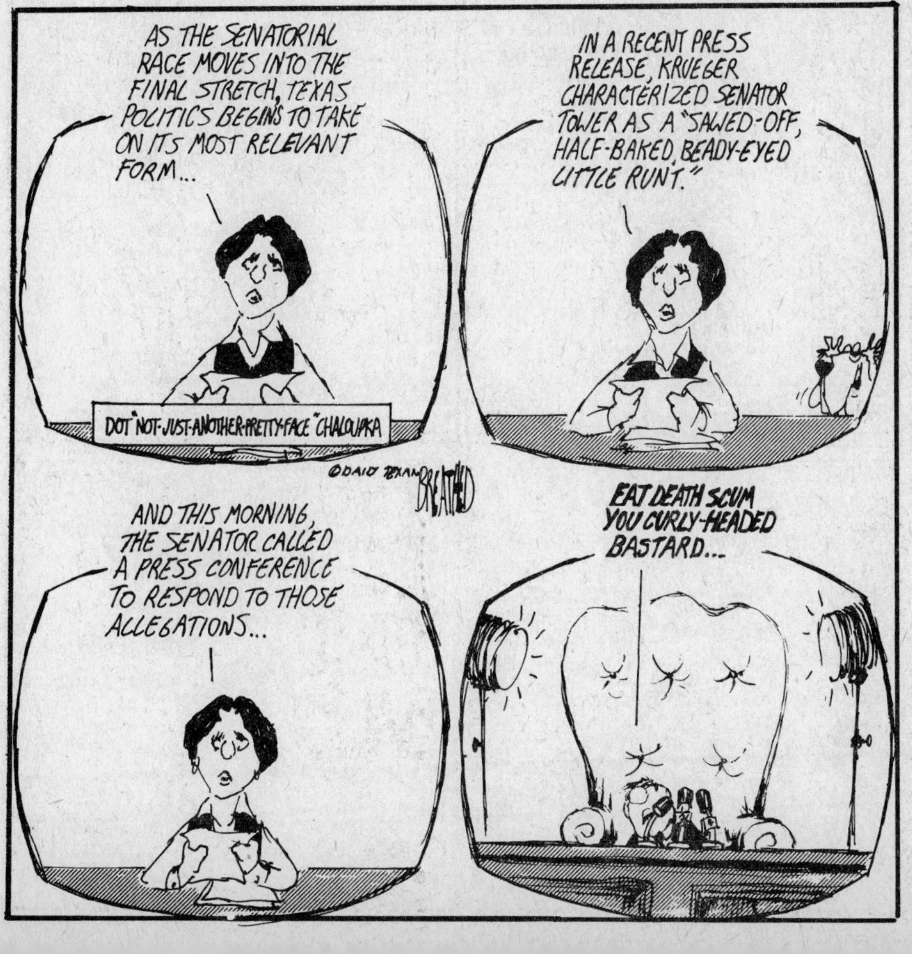
AS THE SENATORIAL RACE MOVES INTO THE FINAL STRETCH, TEXAS POLITICS BEGINS TO TAKE ON ITS MOST RELEVANT FORM...
DOT "NOT-JUST-ANOTHER-PRETTY-FACE" CHALOUPKA
IN A RECENT PRESS RELEASE, KRUEGER CHARACTERIZED SENATOR TOWER AS A "SAWED-OFF, HALF-BAKED, BEADY-EYED LITTLE RUNT."
AND THIS MORNING, THE SENATOR CALLED A PRESS CONFERENCE TO RESPOND TO THOSE ALLEGATIONS...
EAT DEATH SCUM YOU CURLY-HEADED BASTARD...

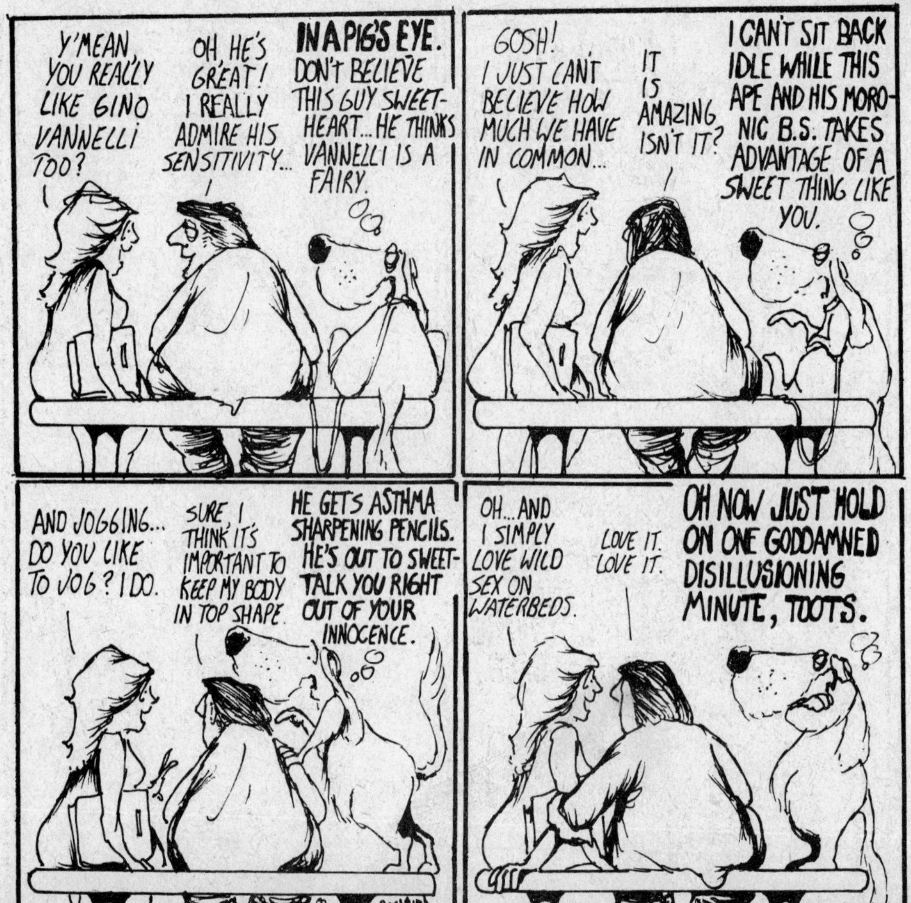

Y'MEAN, YOU REALLY LIKE GINO VANNELLI TOO?
OH, HE'S GREAT! I REALLY ADMIRE HIS SENSITIVITY...
IN A PIG'S EYE. DON'T BELIEVE THIS GUY SWEETHEART... HE THINKS VANNELLI IS A FAIRY.
GOSH! I JUST CAN'T BELIEVE HOW MUCH WE HAVE IN COMMON...
IT IS AMAZING ISN'T IT?
I CAN'T SIT BACK IDLE WHILE THIS APE AND HIS MORONIC B.S. TAKES ADVANTAGE OF A SWEET THING LIKE YOU.
AND JOGGING... DO YOU LIKE TO JOG? I DO.
SURE, I THINK IT'S IMPORTANT TO KEEP MY BODY IN TOP SHAPE.
HE GETS ASTHMA SHARPENING PENCILS. HE'S OUT TO SWEET-TALK YOU RIGHT OUT OF YOUR INNOCENCE.
OH... AND I SIMPLY LOVE WILD SEX ON WATERBEDS.
LOVE IT. LOVE IT.
OH NOW JUST HOLD ON ONE GODDAMNED DISILLUSIONING MINUTE, TOOTS.

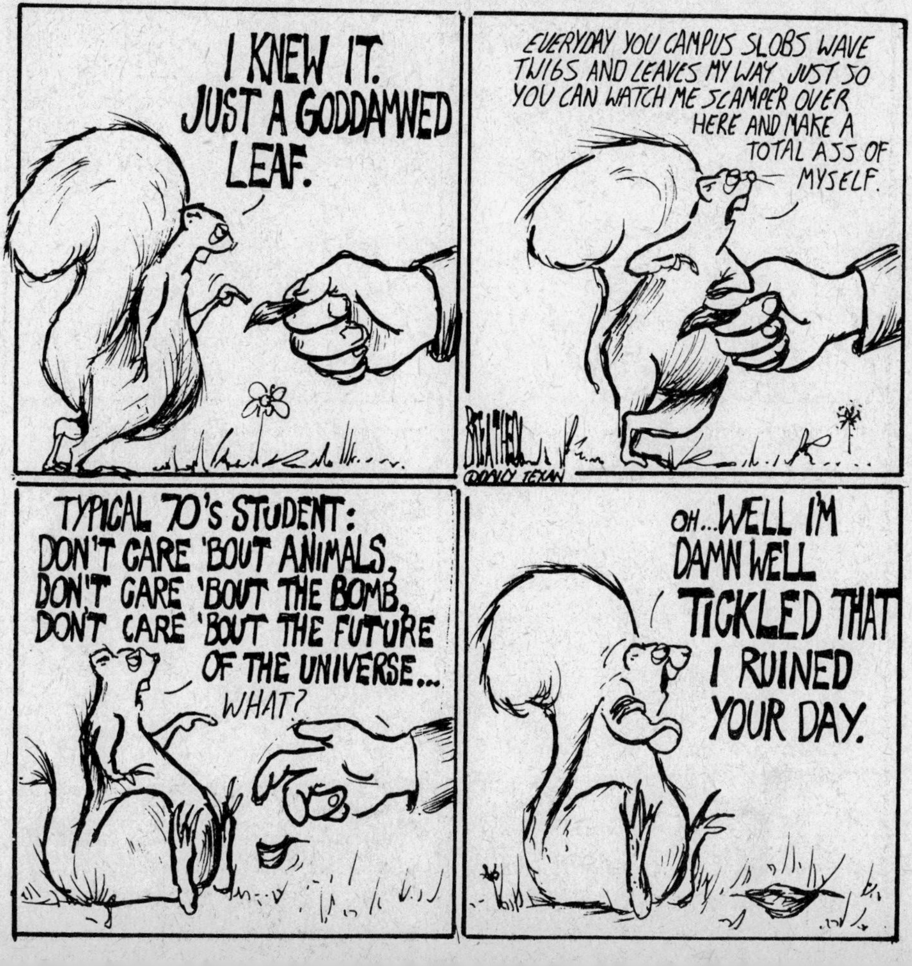
I KNEW IT. JUST A GODDAMNED LEAF.
EVERYDAY YOU CAMPUS SLOBS WAVE TWIGS AND LEAVES MY WAY JUST SO YOU CAN WATCH ME SCAMPER OVER HERE AND MAKE A TOTAL ASS OF MYSELF.
BREATHED
©DAILY TEXAN
TYPICAL 70's STUDENT: DON'T CARE 'BOUT ANIMALS, DON'T CARE 'BOUT THE BOMB, DON'T CARE 'BOUT THE FUTURE OF THE UNIVERSE...
WHAT?
OH...WELL I'M DAMN WELL TICKLED THAT I RUINED YOUR DAY.

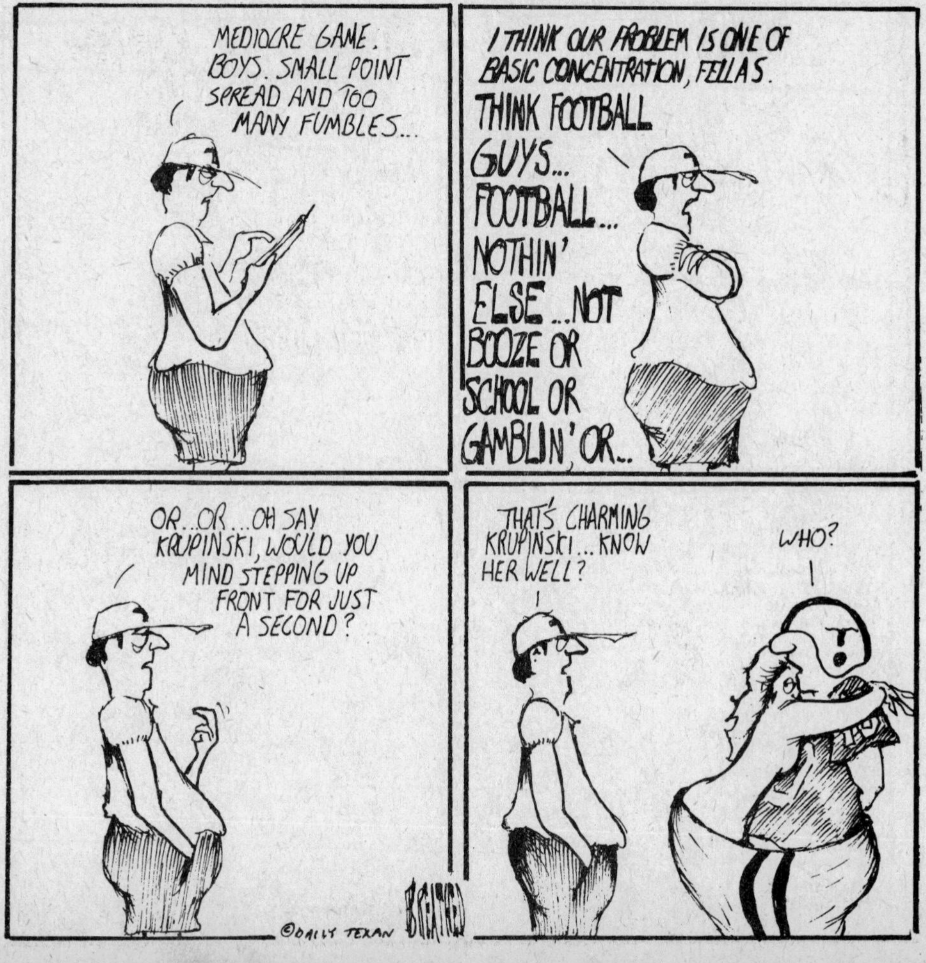

MEDIOCRE GAME. BOYS. SMALL POINT SPREAD AND TOO MANY FUMBLES...
I THINK OUR PROBLEM IS ONE OF BASIC CONCENTRATION, FELLAS.
THINK FOOTBALL GUYS... FOOTBALL... NOTHIN' ELSE ...NOT BOOZE OR SCHOOL OR GAMBLIN', OR...
OR...OR...OH SAY KRUPINSKI, WOULD YOU MIND STEPPING UP FRONT FOR JUST A SECOND?
THAT'S CHARMING KRUPINSKI... KNOW HER WELL?
WHO?
©DAILY TEXAN

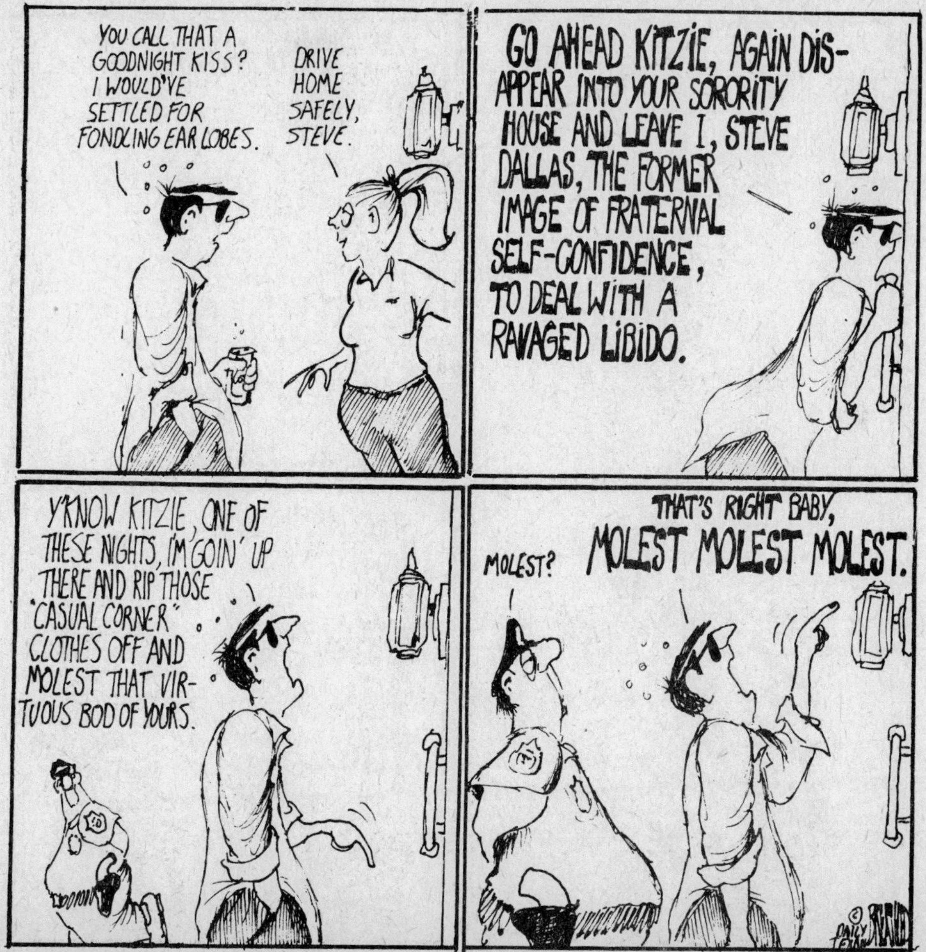
YOU CALL THAT A GOODNIGHT KISS? I WOULD'VE SETTLED FOR FONDLING EAR LOBES.
DRIVE HOME SAFELY, STEVE.
GO AHEAD KITZIE, AGAIN DIS-APPEAR INTO YOUR SORORITY HOUSE AND LEAVE I, STEVE DALLAS, THE FORMER IMAGE OF FRATERNAL SELF-CONFIDENCE, TO DEAL WITH A RAVAGED LIBIDO.
Y'KNOW KITZIE, ONE OF THESE NIGHTS, I'M GOIN' UP THERE AND RIP THOSE "CASUAL CORNER" CLOTHES OFF AND MOLEST THAT VIR-TUOUS BOD OF YOURS.
MOLEST?
THAT'S RIGHT BABY, MOLEST MOLEST MOLEST.

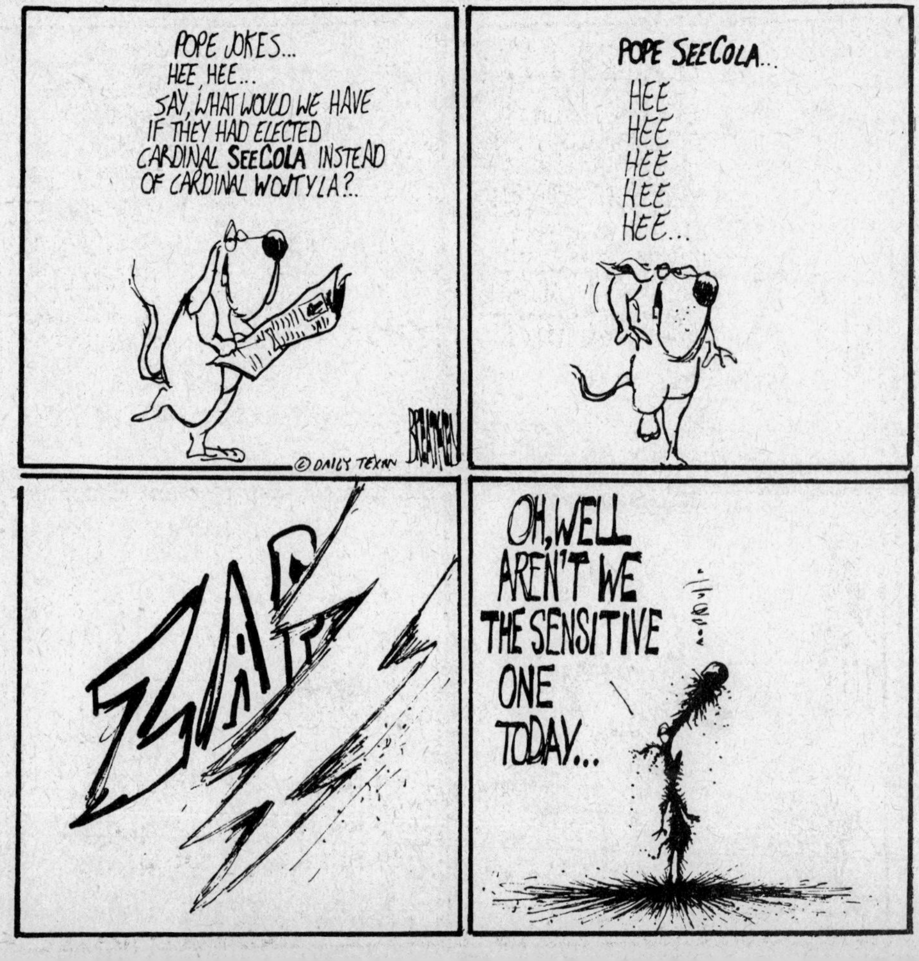
POPE JOKES... HEE HEE... SAY, WHAT WOULD WE HAVE IF THEY HAD ELECTED CARDINAL SEECOLA INSTEAD OF CARDINAL WOJTYLA?..
© DAILY TEXAN
POPE SEECOLA... HEE HEE HEE HEE HEE...
ZAP
OH, WELL AREN'T WE THE SENSITIVE ONE TODAY...

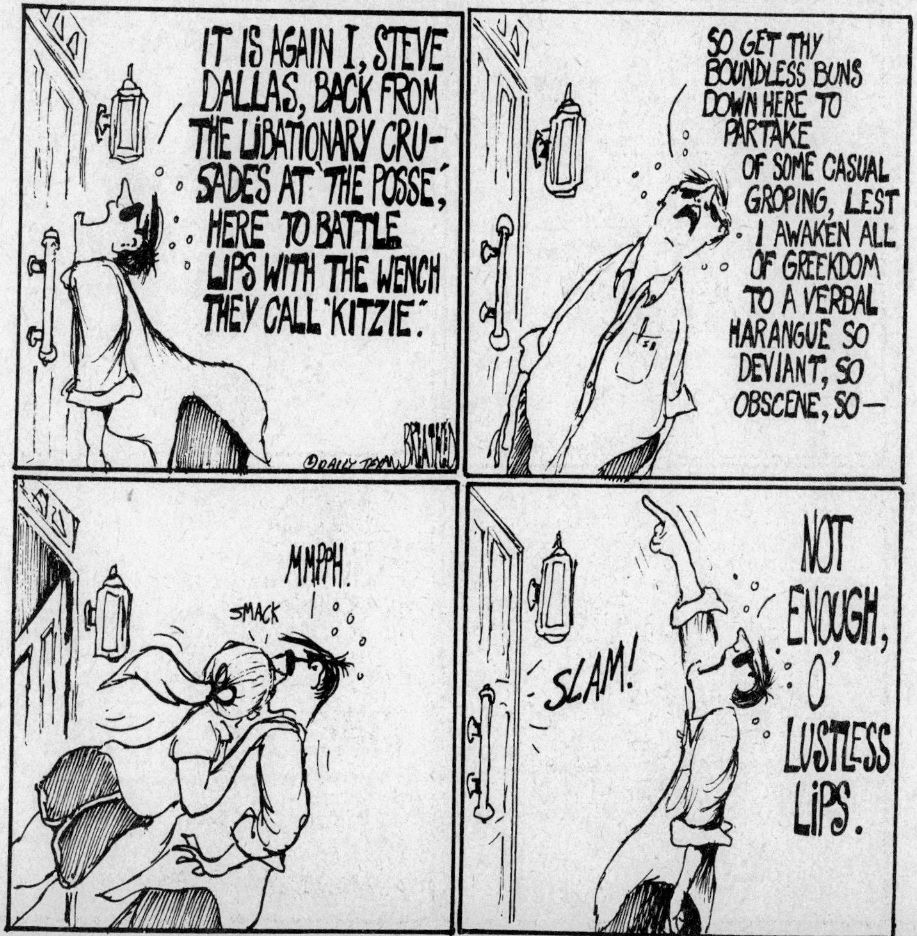
IT IS AGAIN I, STEVE DALLAS, BACK FROM THE LIBATIONARY CRUSADES AT "THE POSSE", HERE TO BATTLE LIPS WITH THE WENCH THEY CALL "KITZIE".
BREATHED
SO GET THY BOUNDLESS BUNS DOWN HERE TO PARTAKE OF SOME CASUAL GROPING, LEST I AWAKEN ALL OF GREEKDOM TO A VERBAL HARANGUE SO DEVIANT, SO OBSCENE, SO—
MMPPH.
SMACK
SLAM!
NOT ENOUGH, O' LUSTLESS LIPS.

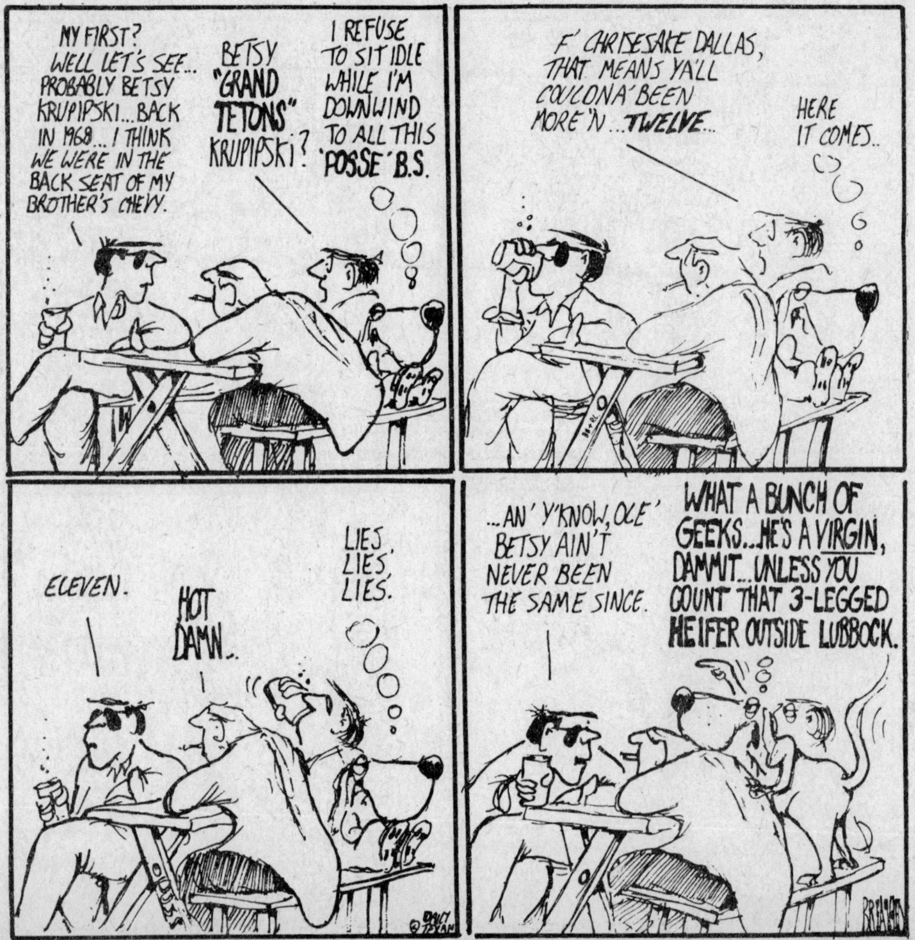

MY FIRST? WELL LET'S SEE... PROBABLY BETSY KRUPIPSKI... BACK IN 1968... I THINK WE WERE IN THE BACK SEAT OF MY BROTHER'S CHEVY.
BETSY "GRAND TETONS" KRUPIPSKI?
I REFUSE TO SIT IDLE WHILE I'M DOWNWIND TO ALL THIS 'POSSE' B.S.
F' CHRISESAKE DALLAS, THAT MEANS YA'LL COULDNA' BEEN MORE 'N ...TWELVE...
HERE IT COMES..
ELEVEN.
HOT DAMN..
LIES, LIES, LIES.
...AN' Y'KNOW, OLE' BETSY AIN'T NEVER BEEN THE SAME SINCE.
WHAT A BUNCH OF GEEKS...HE'S A VIRGIN, DAMMIT...UNLESS YOU COUNT THAT 3-LEGGED HEIFER OUTSIDE LUBBOCK.

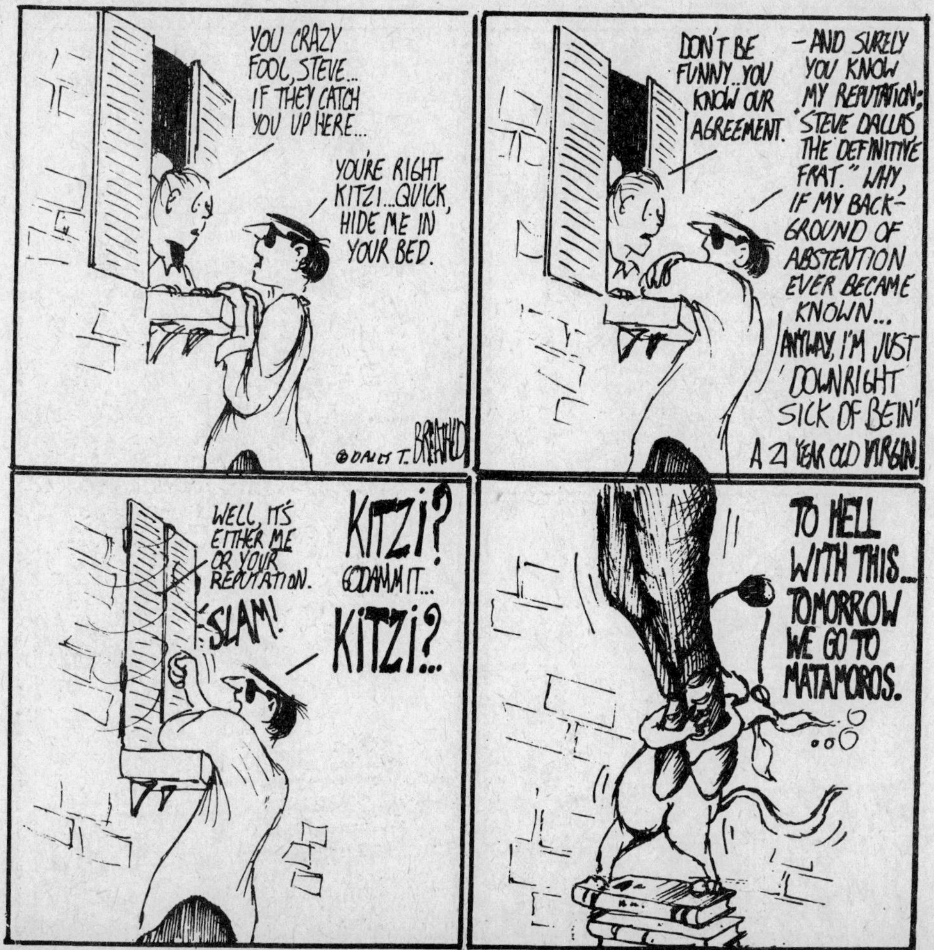
YOU CRAZY FOOL, STEVE... IF THEY CATCH YOU UP HERE...
YOU'RE RIGHT KITZI...QUICK, HIDE ME IN YOUR BED.
DON'T BE FUNNY...YOU KNOW OUR AGREEMENT.
-AND SURELY YOU KNOW MY REPUTATION; "STEVE DALLAS THE DEFINITIVE FRAT." WHY, IF MY BACKGROUND OF ABSTENTION EVER BECAME KNOWN...
ANYWAY, I'M JUST DOWNRIGHT SICK OF BEIN' A 21 YEAR OLD VIRGIN.
WELL, IT'S EITHER ME OR YOUR REPUTATION.
SLAM!
KITZI? GODAMMIT... KITZI?..
TO HELL WITH THIS... TOMORROW WE GO TO MATAMOROS.

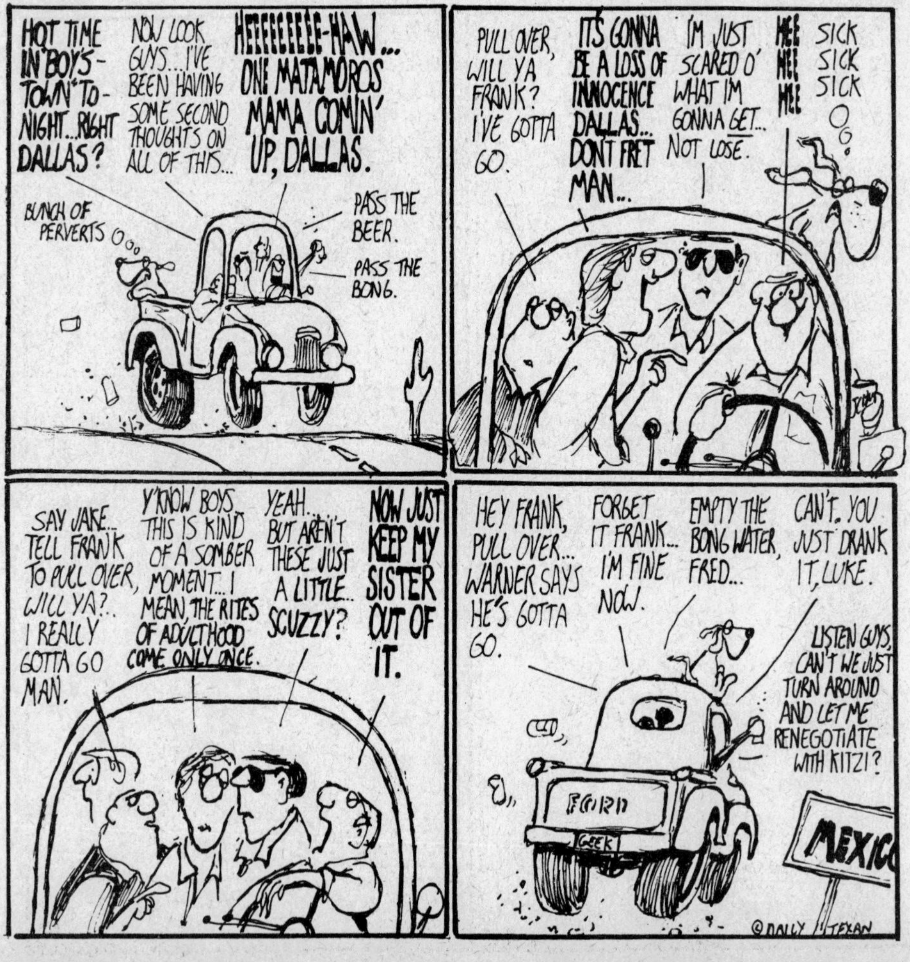
HOT TIME IN "BOY'S-TOWN" TO-NIGHT... RIGHT DALLAS?
NOW LOOK GUYS... I'VE BEEN HAVING SOME SECOND THOUGHTS ON ALL OF THIS...
HEEEEEEEEE-HAW... ONE MATAMOROS MAMA COMIN' UP, DALLAS.
BUNCH OF PERVERTS
PASS THE BEER.
PASS THE BONG.
PULL OVER, WILL YA FRANK? I'VE GOTTA GO.
IT'S GONNA BE A LOSS OF INNOCENCE DALLAS... DON'T FRET MAN...
I'M JUST SCARED O' WHAT I'M GONNA GET... NOT LOSE.
HEE HEE HEE
SICK SICK SICK
SAY JAKE... TELL FRANK TO PULL OVER, WILL YA?.. I REALLY GOTTA GO MAN.
Y'KNOW BOYS THIS IS KIND OF A SOMBER MOMENT... I MEAN, THE RITES OF ADULTHOOD COME ONLY ONCE.
YEAH... BUT AREN'T THESE JUST A LITTLE... SCUZZY?
NOW JUST KEEP MY SISTER OUT OF IT.
HEY FRANK, PULL OVER... WARNER SAYS HE'S GOTTA GO.
FORGET IT FRANK... I'M FINE NOW.
EMPTY THE BONG WATER, FRED...
CAN'T. YOU JUST DRANK IT, LUKE.
LISTEN GUYS, CAN'T WE JUST TURN AROUND AND LET ME RENEGOTIATE WITH KITZI?
FORD
GEEK
MEXICO
© DAILY TEXAN

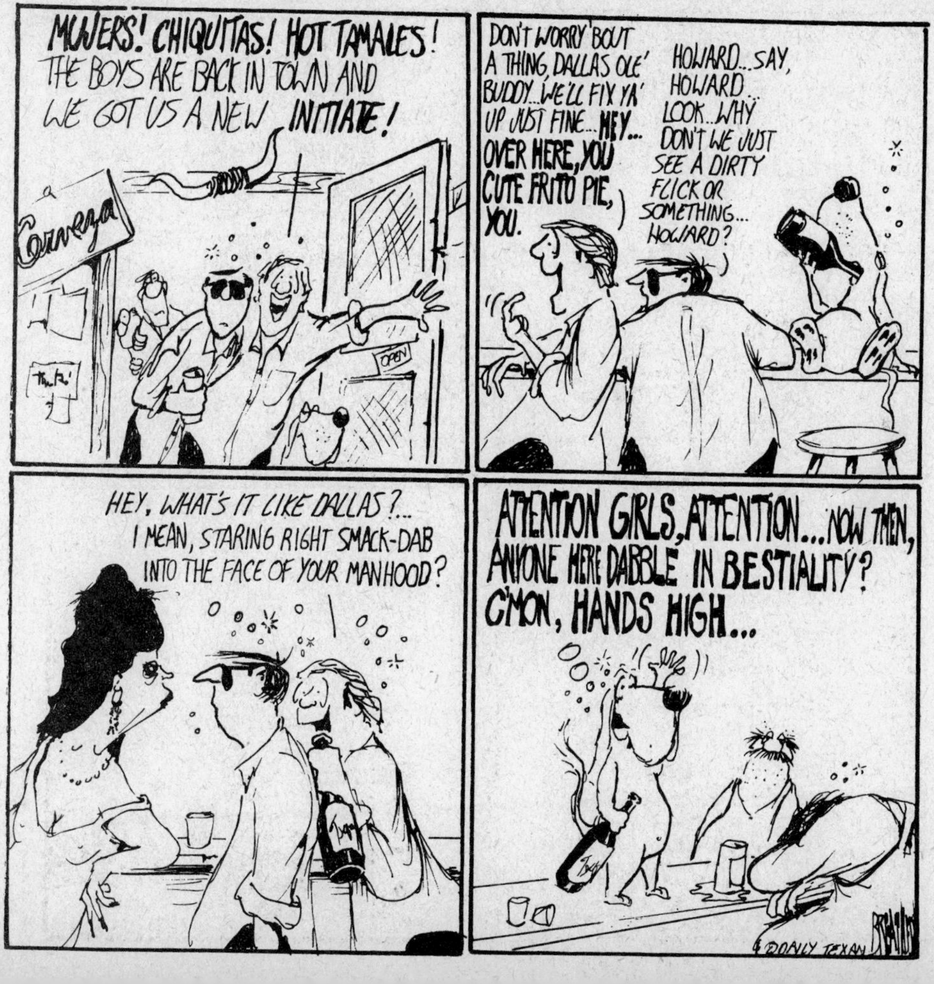
MUJERS! CHIQUITAS! HOT TAMALES!
THE BOYS ARE BACK IN TOWN AND WE GOT US A NEW INITIATE!
Cerveza
OPEN
DON'T WORRY 'BOUT A THING, DALLAS OLE' BUDDY...WE'LL FIX YA' UP JUST FINE...HEY... OVER HERE, YOU CUTE FRITO PIE, YOU.
HOWARD...SAY, HOWARD... LOOK...WHY DON'T WE JUST SEE A DIRTY FLICK OR SOMETHING... HOWARD?
HEY, WHAT'S IT LIKE DALLAS?... I MEAN, STARING RIGHT SMACK-DAB INTO THE FACE OF YOUR MANHOOD?
ATTENTION GIRLS, ATTENTION...NOW THEN, ANYONE HERE DABBLE IN BESTIALITY? C'MON, HANDS HIGH...
©DAILY TEXAN

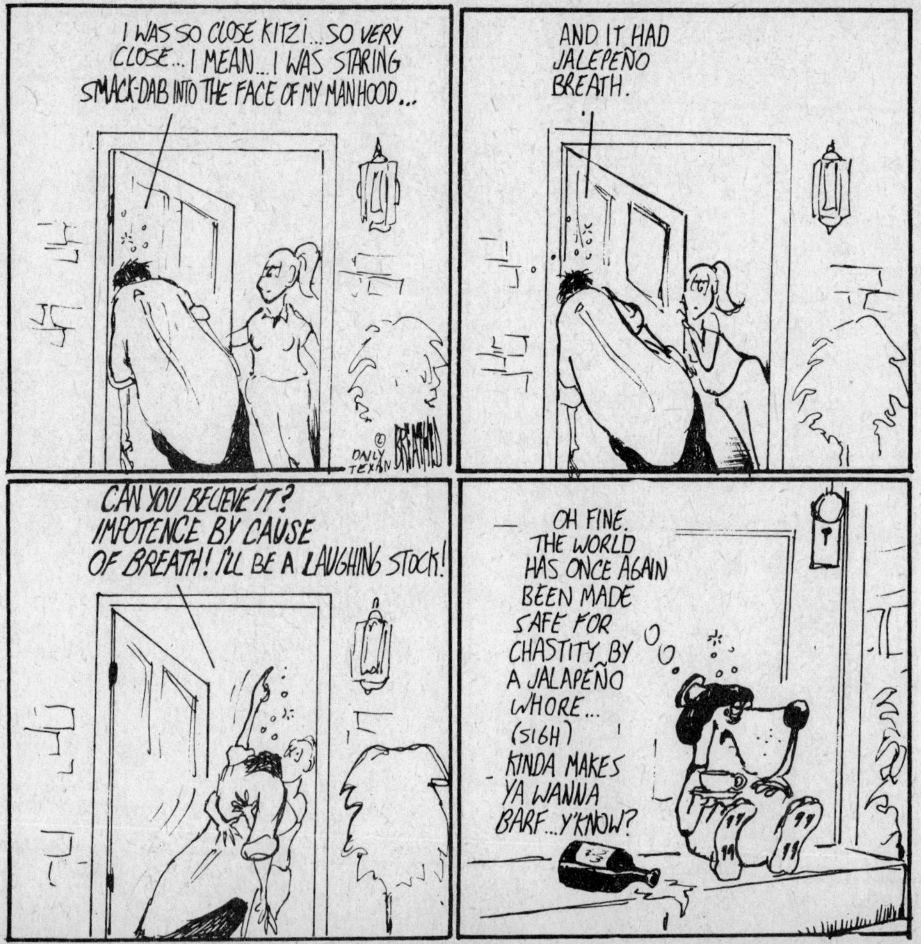
I WAS SO CLOSE KITZI... SO VERY CLOSE... I MEAN... I WAS STARING SMACK-DAB INTO THE FACE OF MY MANHOOD...
© DAILY TEXAN
BREATHED
AND IT HAD JALEPEÑO BREATH.
CAN YOU BELIEVE IT? IMPOTENCE BY CAUSE OF BREATH! I'LL BE A LAUGHING STOCK!
OH FINE. THE WORLD HAS ONCE AGAIN BEEN MADE SAFE FOR CHASTITY BY A JALAPEÑO WHORE... (SIGH) KINDA MAKES YA WANNA BARF... Y'KNOW?

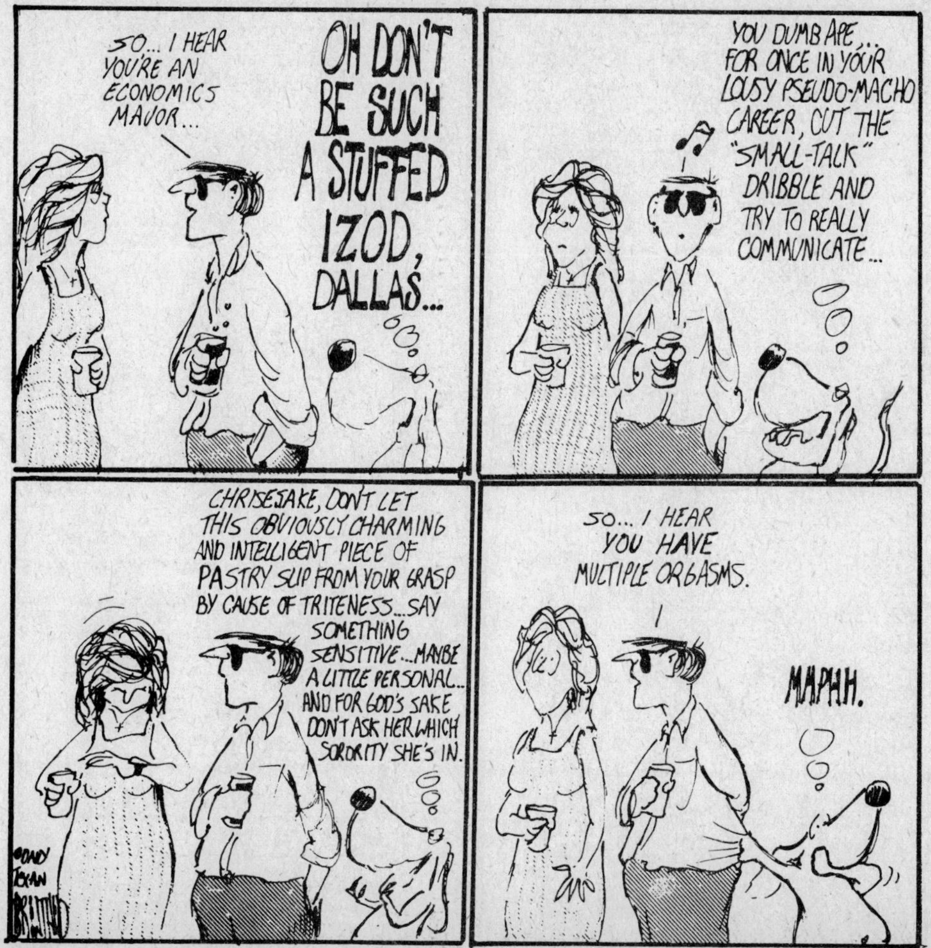
SO... I HEAR YOU'RE AN ECONOMICS MAJOR...
OH DON'T BE SUCH A STUFFED IZOD, DALLAS...
YOU DUMB APE... FOR ONCE IN YOUR LOUSY PSEUDO-MACHO CAREER, CUT THE "SMALL-TALK" DRIBBLE AND TRY TO REALLY COMMUNICATE...
CHRISESAKE, DON'T LET THIS OBVIOUSLY CHARMING AND INTELLIGENT PIECE OF PASTRY SLIP FROM YOUR GRASP BY CAUSE OF TRITENESS...SAY SOMETHING SENSITIVE...MAYBE A LITTLE PERSONAL... AND FOR GOD'S SAKE DON'T ASK HER WHICH SORORITY SHE'S IN.
SO... I HEAR YOU HAVE MULTIPLE ORGASMS.
MAPHH.

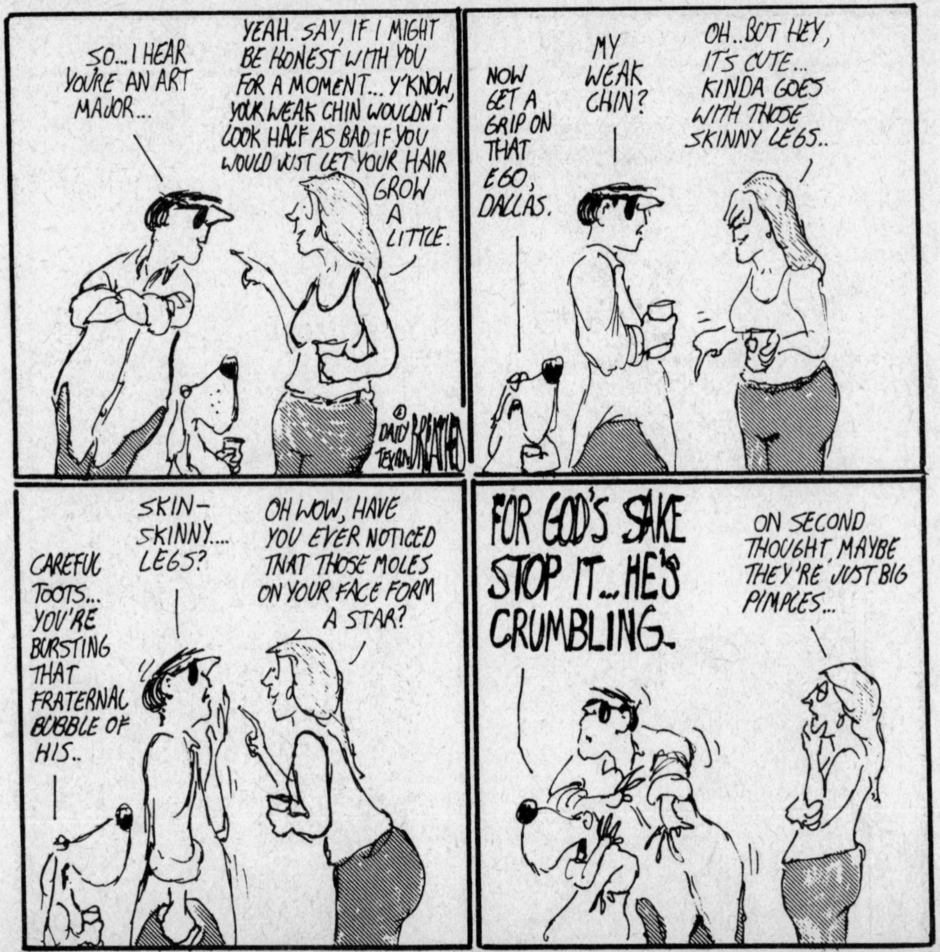
SO... I HEAR YOU'RE AN ART MAJOR...
YEAH. SAY, IF I MIGHT BE HONEST WITH YOU FOR A MOMENT... Y'KNOW, YOUR WEAK CHIN WOULDN'T LOOK HALF AS BAD IF YOU WOULD JUST LET YOUR HAIR GROW A LITTLE.
© DAILY TEXAN BREATHED
NOW GET A GRIP ON THAT EGO, DALLAS.
MY WEAK CHIN?
OH.. BUT HEY, IT'S CUTE... KINDA GOES WITH THOSE SKINNY LEGS..
CAREFUL TOOTS... YOU'RE BURSTING THAT FRATERNAL BUBBLE OF HIS..
SKIN-SKINNY.... LEGS?
OH WOW, HAVE YOU EVER NOTICED THAT THOSE MOLES ON YOUR FACE FORM A STAR?
FOR GOD'S SAKE STOP IT... HE'S CRUMBLING..
ON SECOND THOUGHT, MAYBE THEY'RE JUST BIG PIMPLES...

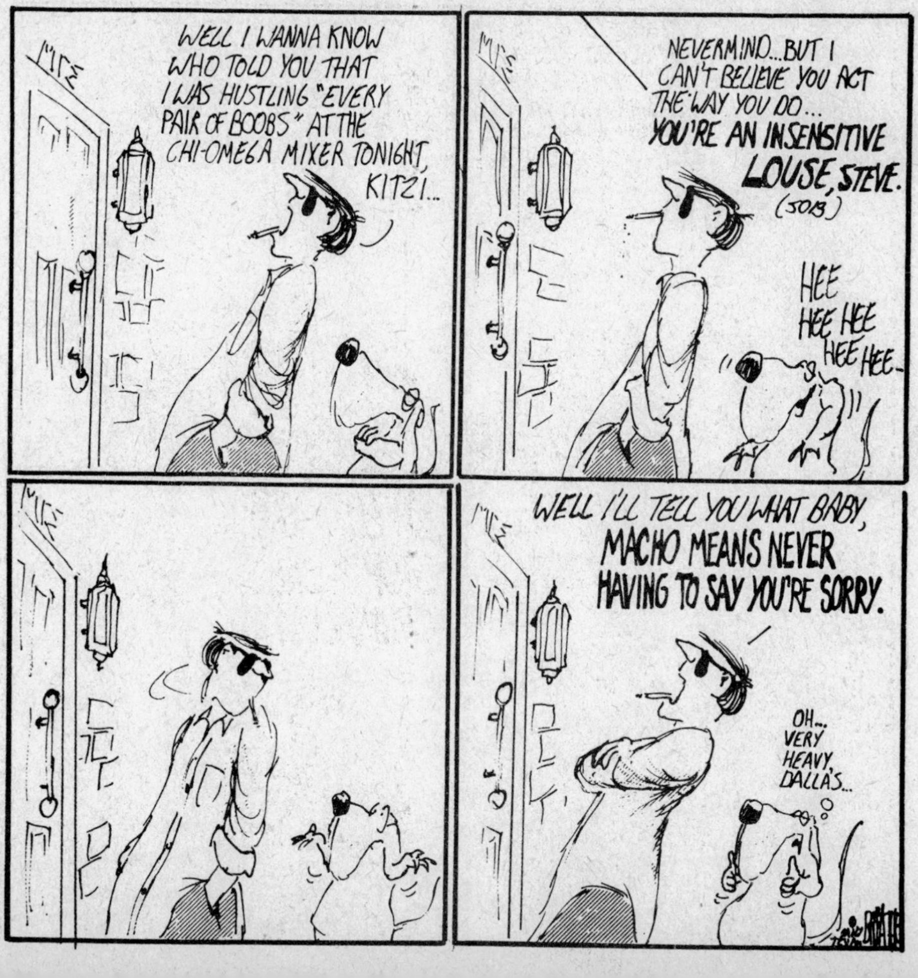
WELL I WANNA KNOW WHO TOLD YOU THAT I WAS HUSTLING "EVERY PAIR OF BOOBS" AT THE CHI-OMEGA MIXER TONIGHT, KITZI...
NEVERMIND...BUT I CAN'T BELIEVE YOU ACT THE WAY YOU DO... YOU'RE AN INSENSITIVE LOUSE, STEVE.
(SOB)
HEE HEE HEE HEE HEE-
WELL I'LL TELL YOU WHAT BABY, MACHO MEANS NEVER HAVING TO SAY YOU'RE SORRY.
OH... VERY HEAVY, DALLAS...

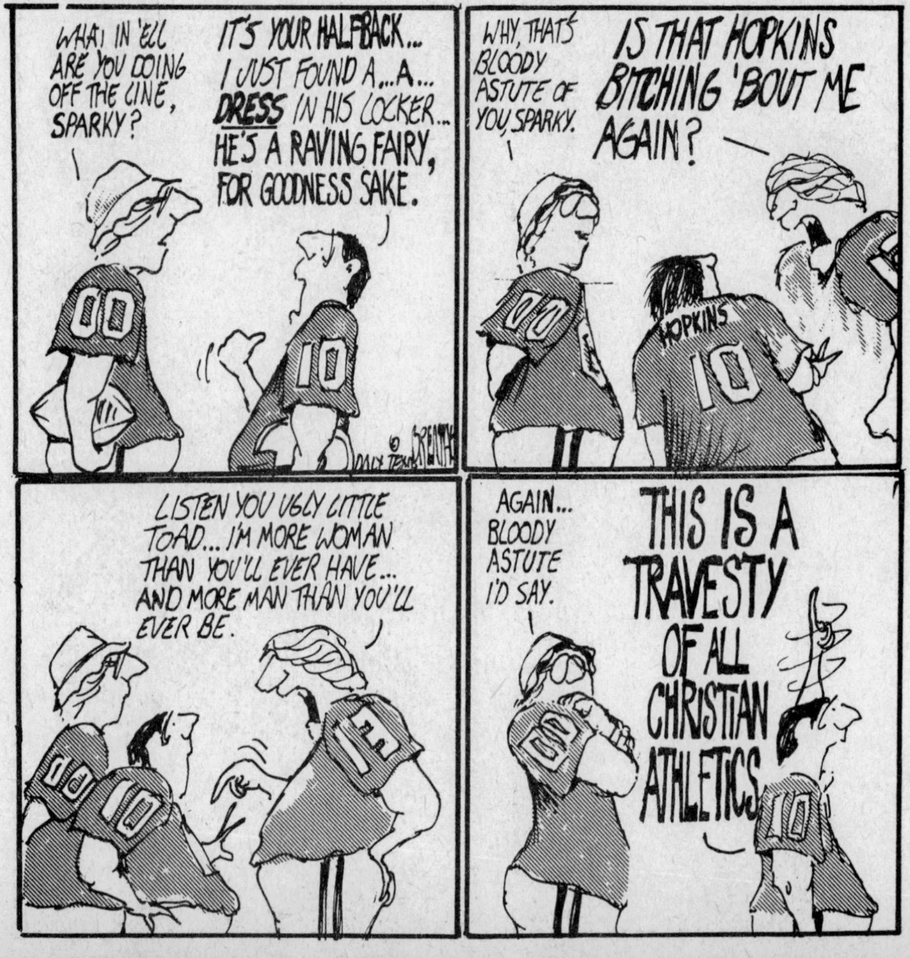

WHAT IN 'ELL ARE YOU DOING OFF THE LINE, SPARKY?
IT'S YOUR HALFBACK... I JUST FOUND A... A... DRESS IN HIS LOCKER... HE'S A RAVING FAIRY, FOR GOODNESS SAKE.
WHY, THAT'S BLOODY ASTUTE OF YOU, SPARKY.
IS THAT HOPKINS BITCHING 'BOUT ME AGAIN?
HOPKINS
LISTEN YOU UGLY LITTLE TOAD... I'M MORE WOMAN THAN YOU'LL EVER HAVE... AND MORE MAN THAN YOU'LL EVER BE.
AGAIN... BLOODY ASTUTE I'D SAY.
THIS IS A TRAVESTY OF ALL CHRISTIAN ATHLETICS

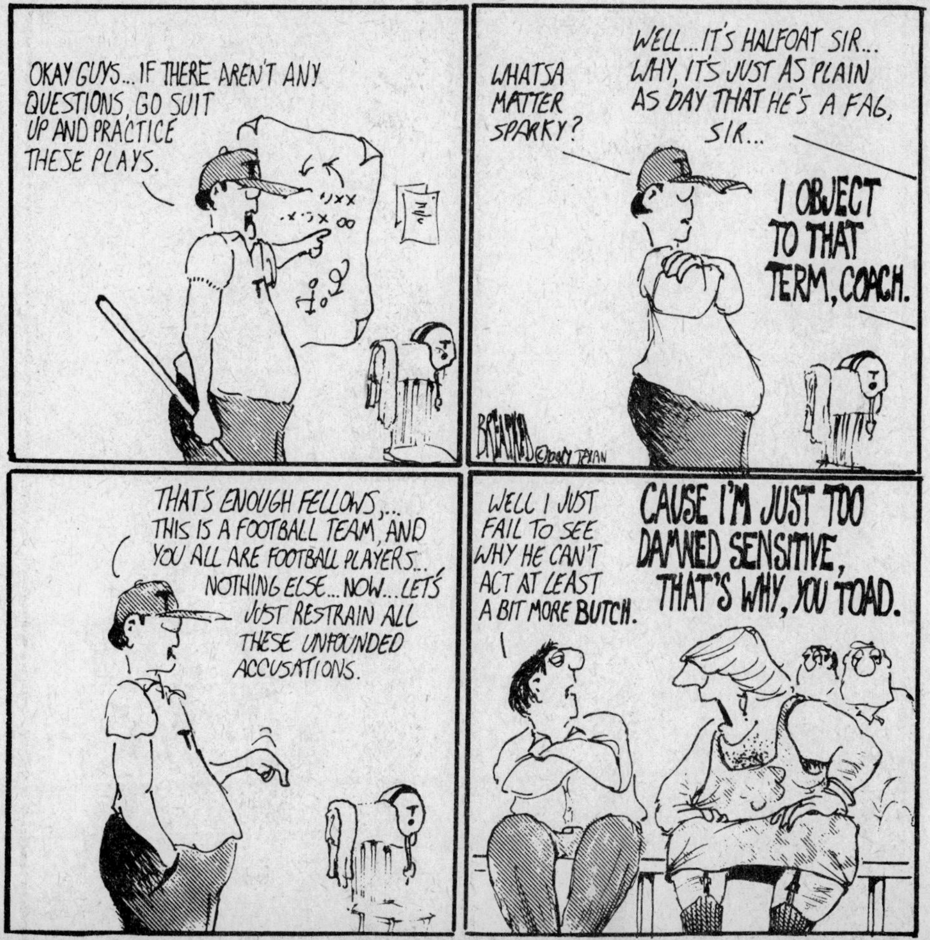
OKAY GUYS... IF THERE AREN'T ANY QUESTIONS, GO SUIT UP AND PRACTICE THESE PLAYS.
WHATSA MATTER SPARKY?
WELL... IT'S HALFOAT SIR... WHY, IT'S JUST AS PLAIN AS DAY THAT HE'S A FAG, SIR...
I OBJECT TO THAT TERM, COACH.
THAT'S ENOUGH FELLOWS,... THIS IS A FOOTBALL TEAM, AND YOU ALL ARE FOOTBALL PLAYERS... NOTHING ELSE... NOW... LET'S JUST RESTRAIN ALL THESE UNFOUNDED ACCUSATIONS.
WELL I JUST FAIL TO SEE WHY HE CAN'T ACT AT LEAST A BIT MORE BUTCH.
CAUSE I'M JUST TOO DAMNED SENSITIVE, THAT'S WHY, YOU TOAD.

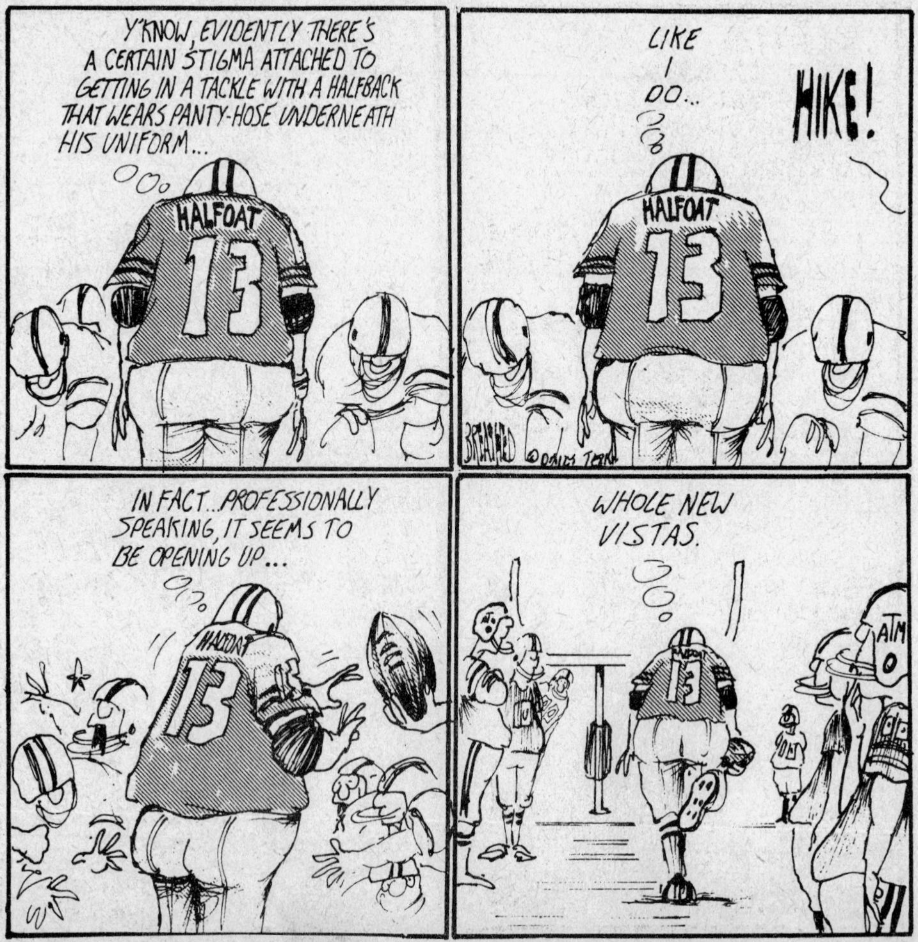

Y'KNOW, EVIDENTLY THERE'S A CERTAIN STIGMA ATTACHED TO GETTING IN A TACKLE WITH A HALFBACK THAT WEARS PANTY-HOSE UNDERNEATH HIS UNIFORM...
HALFOAT
13
LIKE I DO...
HIKE!
HALFOAT
13
IN FACT...PROFESSIONALLY SPEAKING, IT SEEMS TO BE OPENING UP...
13
WHOLE NEW VISTAS.
13

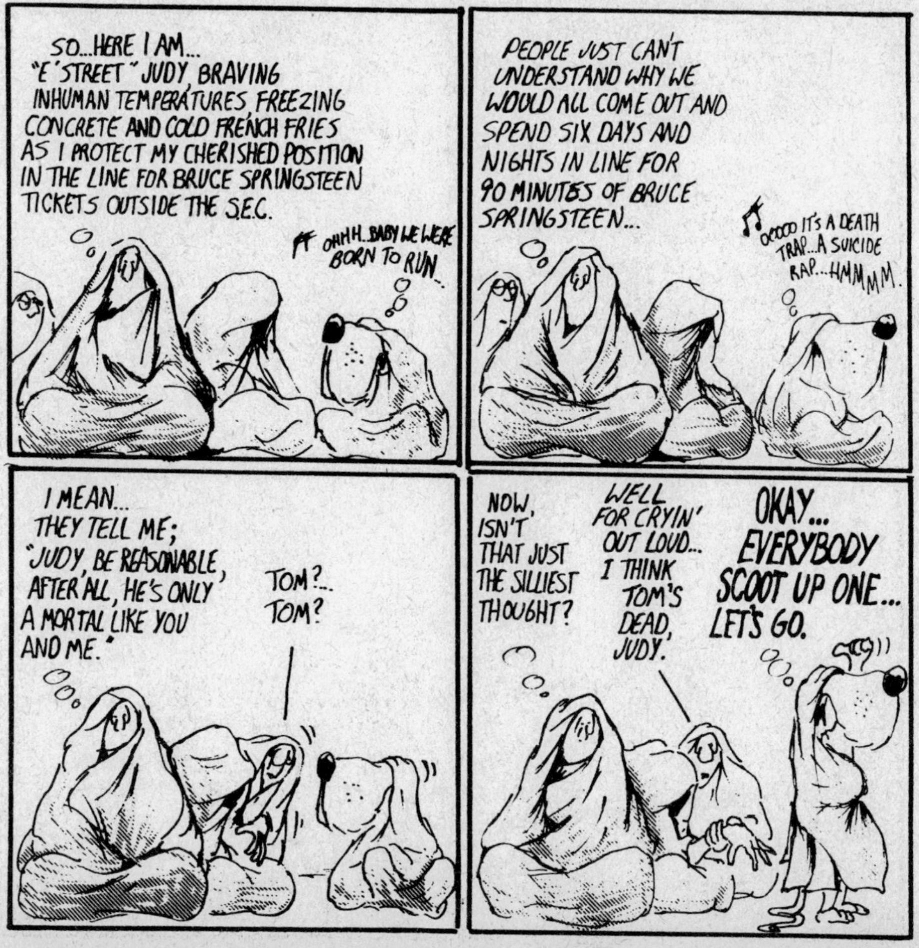
SO...HERE I AM...
"E STREET" JUDY, BRAVING INHUMAN TEMPERATURES, FREEZING CONCRETE AND COLD FRENCH FRIES AS I PROTECT MY CHERISHED POSITION IN THE LINE FOR BRUCE SPRINGSTEEN TICKETS OUTSIDE THE S.E.C.
OHHH..BABY WE WERE BORN TO RUN...
PEOPLE JUST CAN'T UNDERSTAND WHY WE WOULD ALL COME OUT AND SPEND SIX DAYS AND NIGHTS IN LINE FOR 90 MINUTES OF BRUCE SPRINGSTEEN...
OOOOO IT'S A DEATH TRAP...A SUICIDE RAP...HMMMMM.
I MEAN... THEY TELL ME; "JUDY, BE REASONABLE, AFTER ALL, HE'S ONLY A MORTAL LIKE YOU AND ME."
TOM?... TOM?
NOW, ISN'T THAT JUST THE SILLIEST THOUGHT?
WELL FOR CRYIN' OUT LOUD... I THINK TOM'S DEAD, JUDY.
OKAY... EVERYBODY SCOOT UP ONE... LET'S GO.

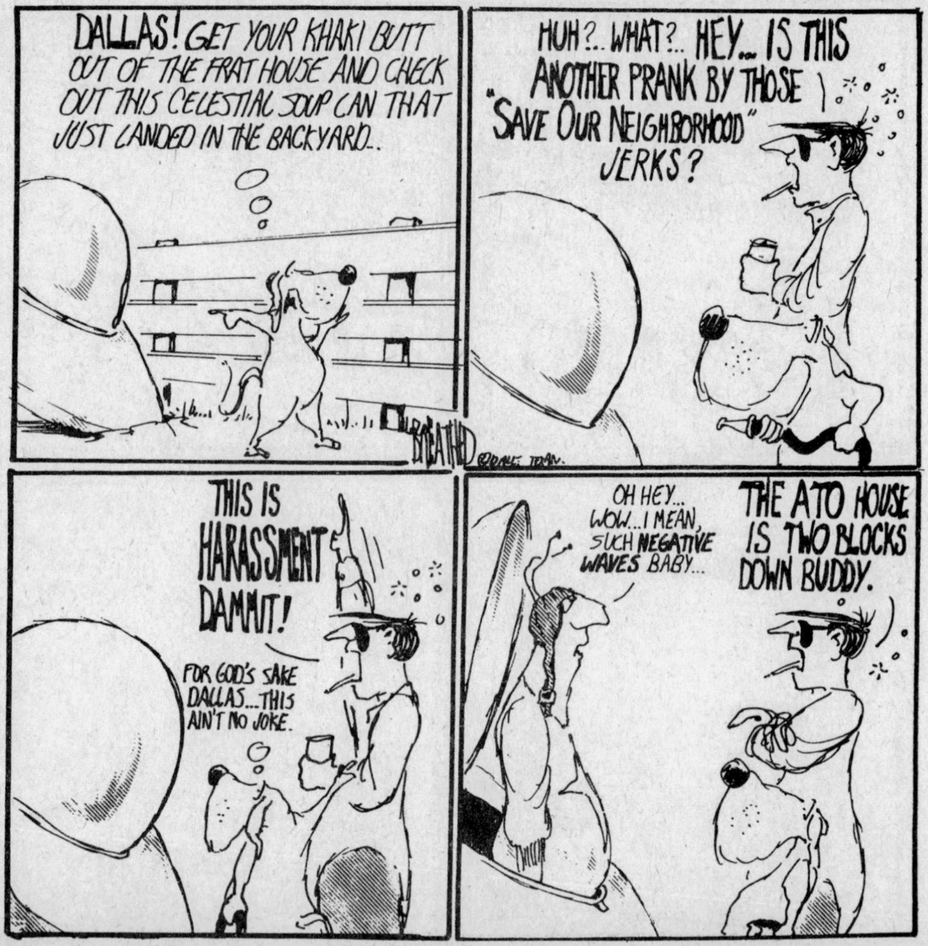
DALLAS! GET YOUR KHAKI BUTT OUT OF THE FRAT HOUSE AND CHECK OUT THIS CELESTIAL SOUP CAN THAT JUST LANDED IN THE BACKYARD..
HUH?.. WHAT?.. HEY... IS THIS ANOTHER PRANK BY THOSE "SAVE OUR NEIGHBORHOOD" JERKS?
BREATHED
THIS IS HARASSMENT DAMMIT!
FOR GOD'S SAKE DALLAS... THIS AIN'T NO JOKE.
OH HEY... WOW... I MEAN, SUCH NEGATIVE WAVES BABY...
THE ATO HOUSE IS TWO BLOCKS DOWN BUDDY.

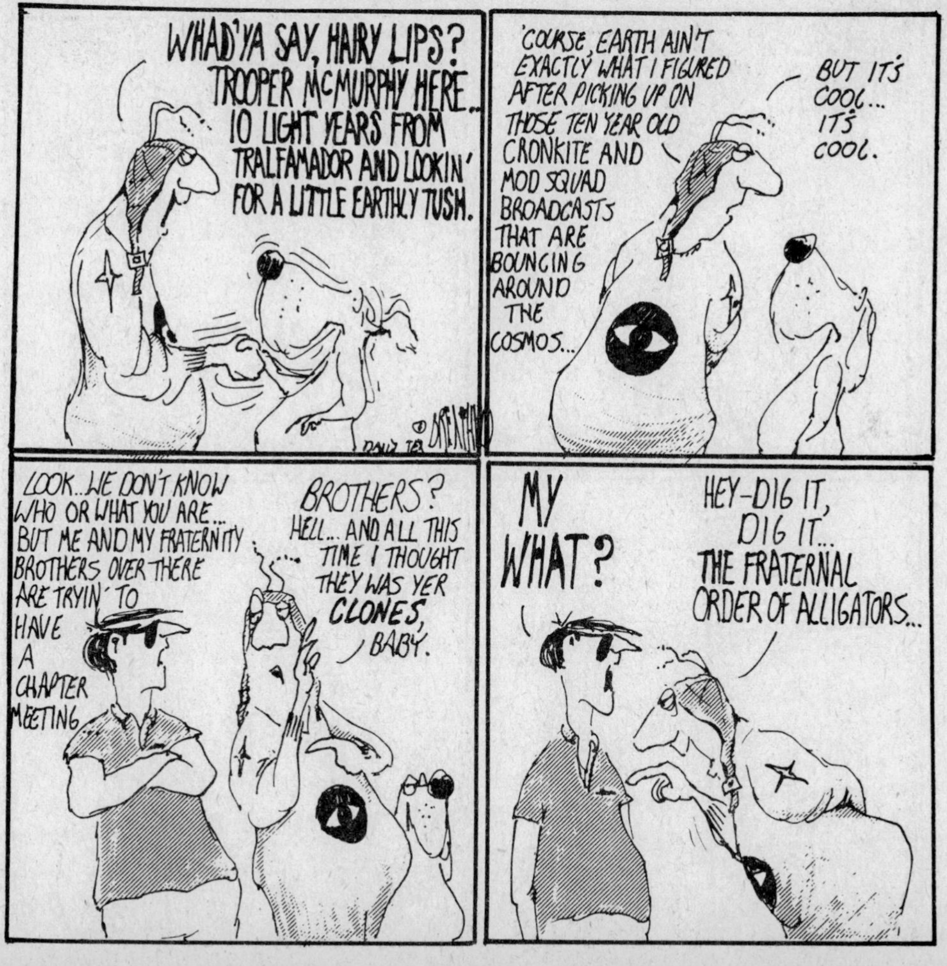
WHAD'YA SAY, HAIRY LIPS? TROOPER McMURPHY HERE... 10 LIGHT YEARS FROM TRALFAMADOR AND LOOKIN' FOR A LITTLE EARTHLY TUSH.
'COURSE, EARTH AIN'T EXACTLY WHAT I FIGURED AFTER PICKING UP ON THOSE TEN YEAR OLD CRONKITE AND MOD SQUAD BROADCASTS THAT ARE BOUNCING AROUND THE COSMOS...
BUT IT'S COOL... IT'S COOL.
LOOK... WE DON'T KNOW WHO OR WHAT YOU ARE... BUT ME AND MY FRATERNITY BROTHERS OVER THERE ARE TRYIN' TO HAVE A CHAPTER MEETING
BROTHERS? HELL... AND ALL THIS TIME I THOUGHT THEY WAS YER CLONES, BABY.
MY WHAT?
HEY-DIG IT, DIG IT... THE FRATERNAL ORDER OF ALLIGATORS...

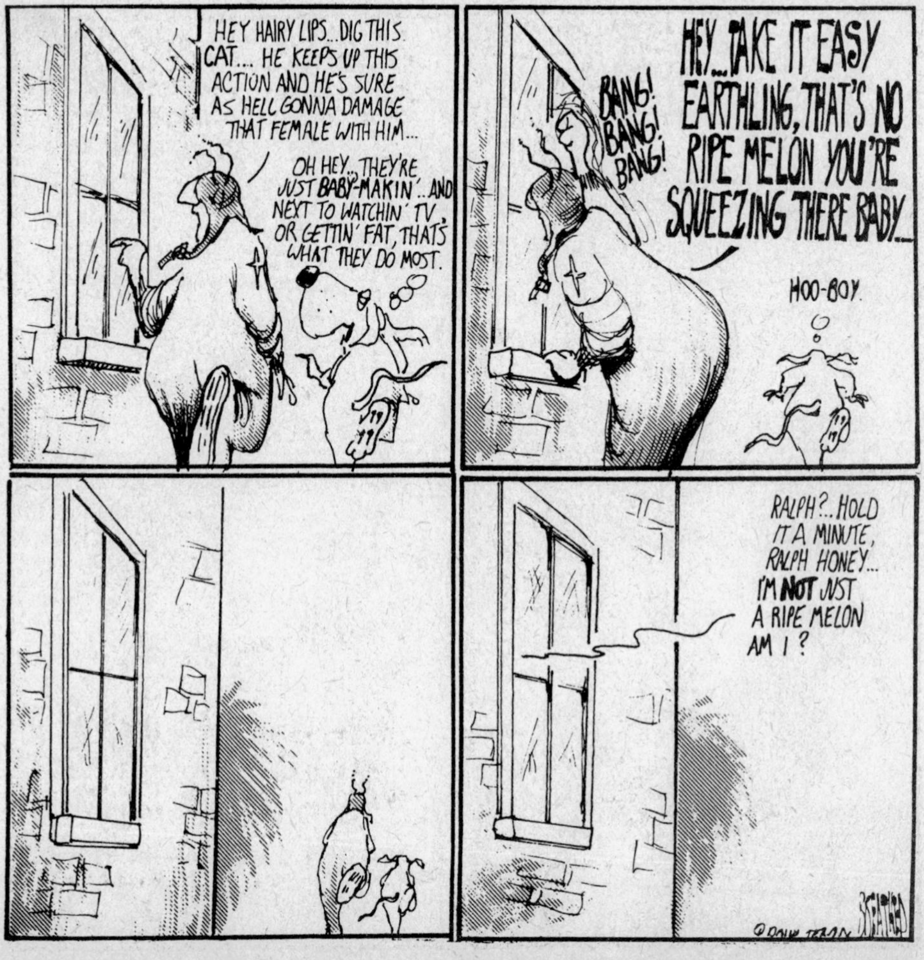

HEY HAIRY LIPS... DIG THIS CAT.... HE KEEPS UP THIS ACTION AND HE'S SURE AS HELL GONNA DAMAGE THAT FEMALE WITH HIM...
OH HEY... THEY'RE JUST BABY-MAKIN'... AND NEXT TO WATCHIN' TV, OR GETTIN' FAT, THAT'S WHAT THEY DO MOST.
BANG! BANG! BANG!
HEY... TAKE IT EASY EARTHLING, THAT'S NO RIPE MELON YOU'RE SQUEEZING THERE BABY...
HOO-BOY.
RALPH?.. HOLD IT A MINUTE, RALPH HONEY... I'M NOT JUST A RIPE MELON AM I?

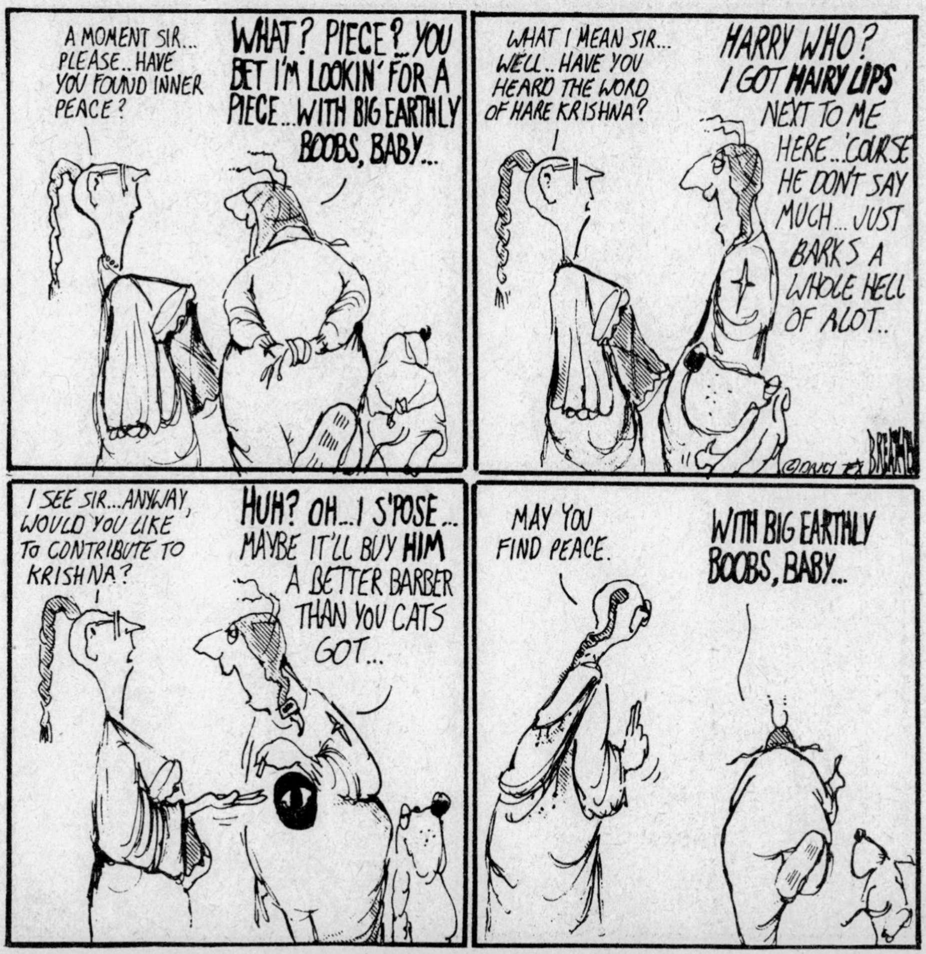
A MOMENT SIR... PLEASE.. HAVE YOU FOUND INNER PEACE?
WHAT? PIECE?...YOU BET I'M LOOKIN' FOR A PIECE...WITH BIG EARTHLY BOOBS, BABY...
WHAT I MEAN SIR... WELL.. HAVE YOU HEARD THE WORD OF HARE KRISHNA?
HARRY WHO? I GOT HAIRY LIPS NEXT TO ME HERE...'COURSE HE DON'T SAY MUCH... JUST BARKS A WHOLE HELL OF ALOT..
I SEE SIR...ANYWAY, WOULD YOU LIKE TO CONTRIBUTE TO KRISHNA?
HUH? OH...I S'POSE... MAYBE IT'LL BUY HIM A BETTER BARBER THAN YOU CATS GOT...
MAY YOU FIND PEACE.
WITH BIG EARTHLY BOOBS, BABY...

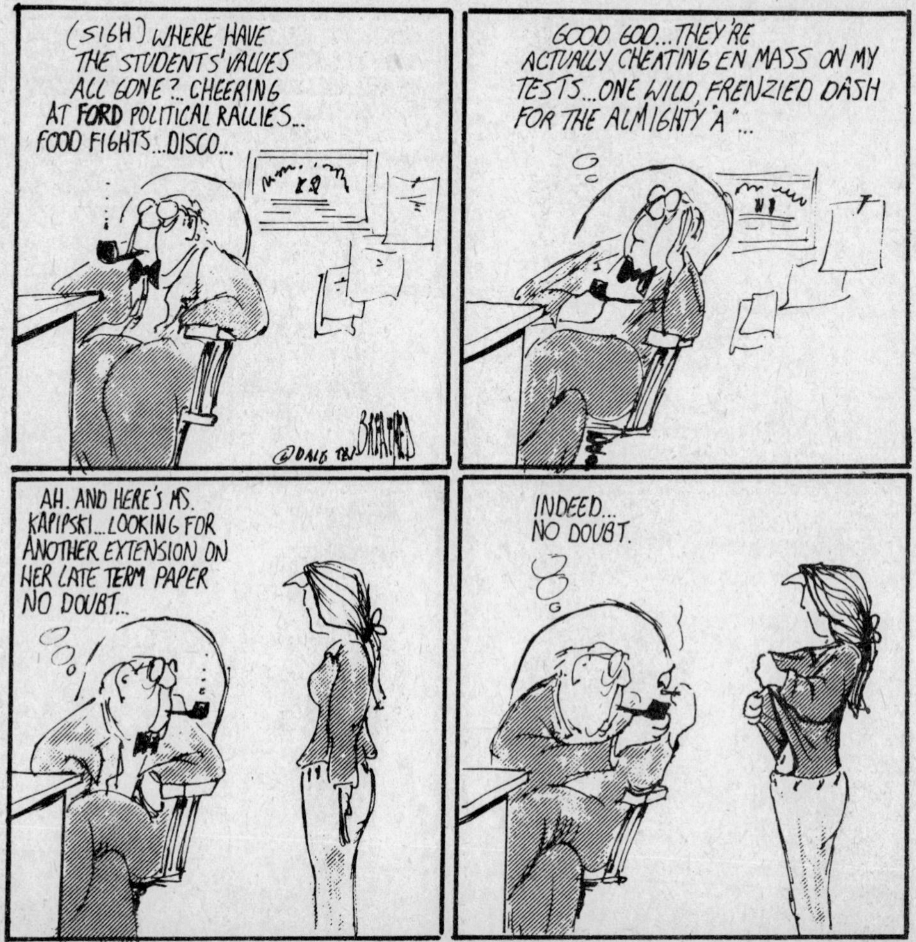
(SIGH) WHERE HAVE THE STUDENTS' VALUES ALL GONE?... CHEERING AT FORD POLITICAL RALLIES... FOOD FIGHTS...DISCO...
GOOD GOD...THEY'RE ACTUALLY CHEATING EN MASS ON MY TESTS...ONE WILD, FRENZIED DASH FOR THE ALMIGHTY "A"...
AH. AND HERE'S MS. KAPIPSKI...LOOKING FOR ANOTHER EXTENSION ON HER LATE TERM PAPER NO DOUBT...
INDEED... NO DOUBT.

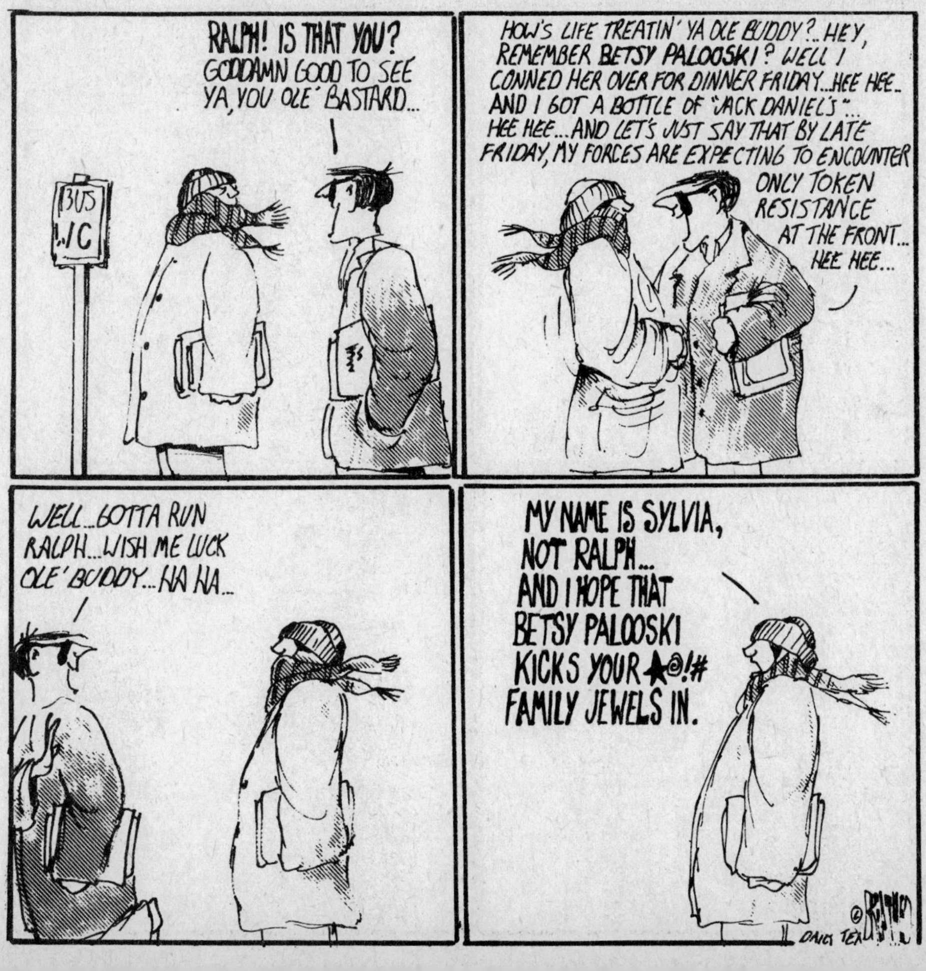
BUS
RALPH! IS THAT YOU? GODDAMN GOOD TO SEE YA, YOU OLE' BASTARD...
HOW'S LIFE TREATIN' YA OLE BUDDY?.. HEY, REMEMBER BETSY PALOOSKI? WELL I CONNED HER OVER FOR DINNER FRIDAY...HEE HEE.. AND I GOT A BOTTLE OF "JACK DANIEL'S"... HEE HEE... AND LET'S JUST SAY THAT BY LATE FRIDAY, MY FORCES ARE EXPECTING TO ENCOUNTER ONLY TOKEN RESISTANCE AT THE FRONT... HEE HEE...
WELL...GOTTA RUN RALPH...WISH ME LUCK OLE' BUDDY...HA HA...
MY NAME IS SYLVIA, NOT RALPH... AND I HOPE THAT BETSY PALOOSKI KICKS YOUR ★@!# FAMILY JEWELS IN.

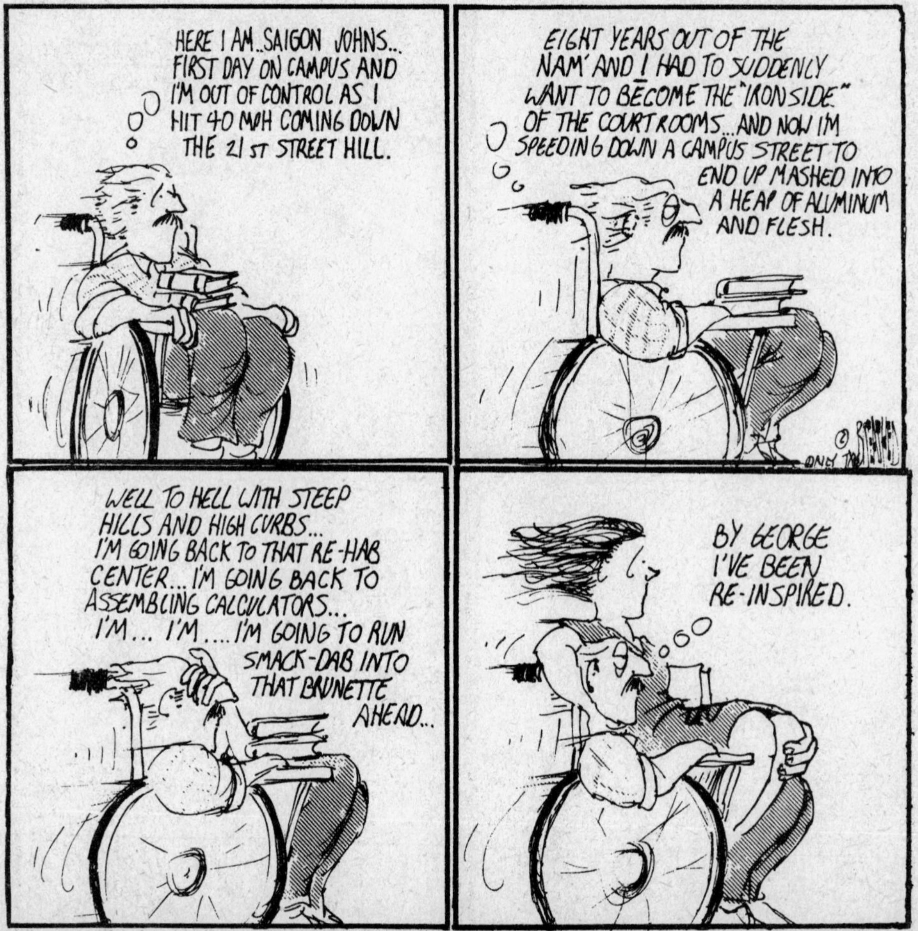
HERE I AM..SAIGON JOHNS... FIRST DAY ON CAMPUS AND I'M OUT OF CONTROL AS I HIT 40 MPH COMING DOWN THE 21 ST STREET HILL.
EIGHT YEARS OUT OF THE NAM' AND I HAD TO SUDDENLY WANT TO BECOME THE "IRONSIDE" OF THE COURTROOMS...AND NOW I'M SPEEDING DOWN A CAMPUS STREET TO END UP MASHED INTO A HEAP OF ALUMINUM AND FLESH.
WELL TO HELL WITH STEEP HILLS AND HIGH CURBS... I'M GOING BACK TO THAT RE-HAB CENTER... I'M GOING BACK TO ASSEMBLING CALCULATORS... I'M... I'M.... I'M GOING TO RUN SMACK-DAB INTO THAT BRUNETTE AHEAD...
BY GEORGE I'VE BEEN RE-INSPIRED.

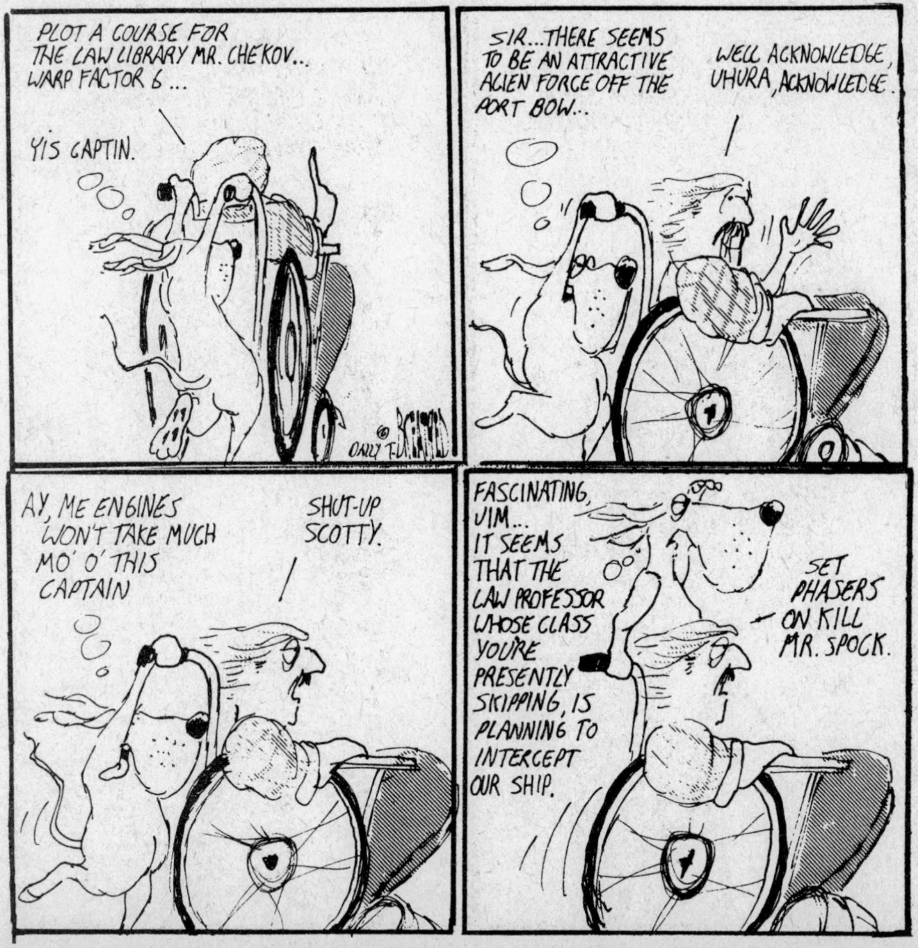
PLOT A COURSE FOR THE LAW LIBRARY MR. CHEKOV... WARP FACTOR 6 ...
YIS CAPTIN.
© ONLY T.
SIR...THERE SEEMS TO BE AN ATTRACTIVE ALIEN FORCE OFF THE PORT BOW...
WELL ACKNOWLEDGE, UHURA, ACKNOWLEDGE.
AY, ME ENGINES WON'T TAKE MUCH MO' O' THIS CAPTAIN
SHUT-UP SCOTTY.
FASCINATING, JIM... IT SEEMS THAT THE LAW PROFESSOR WHOSE CLASS YOU'RE PRESENTLY SKIPPING, IS PLANNING TO INTERCEPT OUR SHIP.
SET PHASERS ON KILL MR. SPOCK.

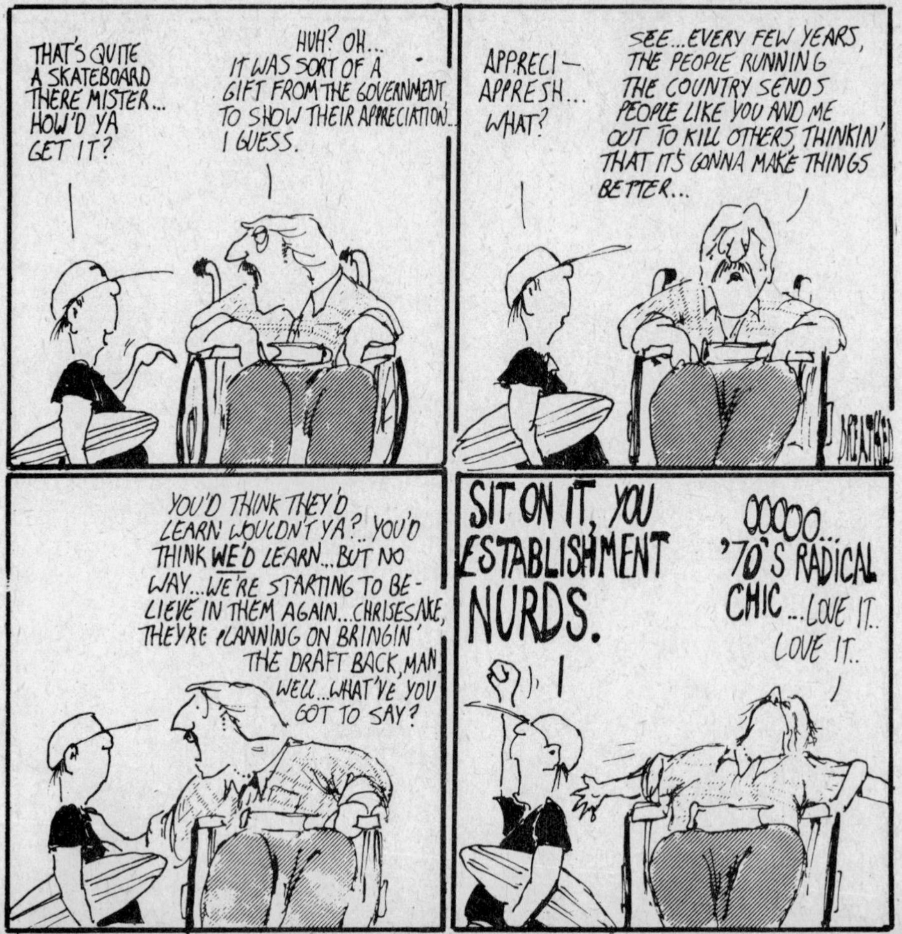
THAT'S QUITE A SKATEBOARD THERE MISTER... HOW'D YA GET IT?
HUH? OH... IT WAS SORT OF A GIFT FROM THE GOVERNMENT TO SHOW THEIR APPRECIATION... I GUESS.
APPRECI– APPRESH... WHAT?
SEE... EVERY FEW YEARS, THE PEOPLE RUNNING THE COUNTRY SENDS PEOPLE LIKE YOU AND ME OUT TO KILL OTHERS, THINKIN' THAT IT'S GONNA MAKE THINGS BETTER...
BREATHED
YOU'D THINK THEY'D LEARN WOULDN'T YA?.. YOU'D THINK WE'D LEARN... BUT NO WAY... WE'RE STARTING TO BELIEVE IN THEM AGAIN... CHRISESAKE, THEY'RE PLANNING ON BRINGIN' THE DRAFT BACK, MAN
WELL... WHAT'VE YOU GOT TO SAY?
SIT ON IT, YOU ESTABLISHMENT NURDS.
OOOOO... '70'S RADICAL CHIC... LOVE IT.. LOVE IT..

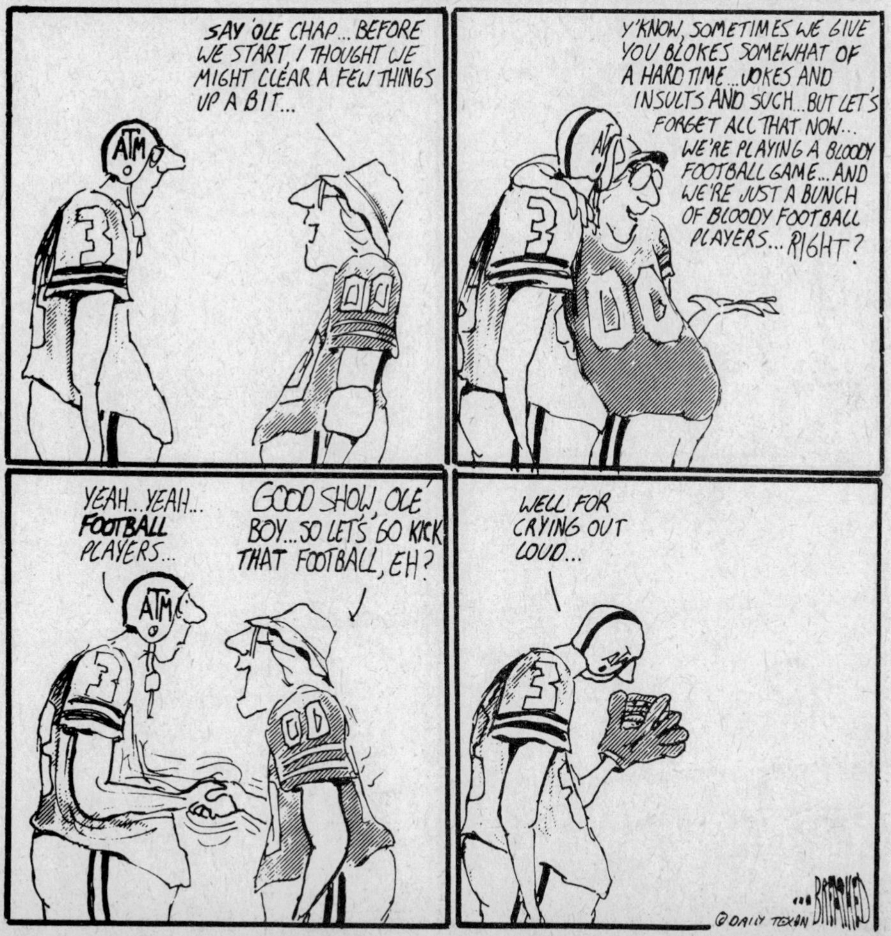
SAY 'OLE CHAP... BEFORE WE START, I THOUGHT WE MIGHT CLEAR A FEW THINGS UP A BIT...
Y'KNOW, SOMETIMES WE GIVE YOU BLOKES SOMEWHAT OF A HARD TIME... JOKES AND INSULTS AND SUCH... BUT LET'S FORGET ALL THAT NOW... WE'RE PLAYING A BLOODY FOOTBALL GAME... AND WE'RE JUST A BUNCH OF BLOODY FOOTBALL PLAYERS... RIGHT?
YEAH... YEAH... FOOTBALL PLAYERS...
GOOD SHOW, OLE' BOY... SO LET'S GO KICK THAT FOOTBALL, EH?
WELL FOR CRYING OUT LOUD...
ATM
©DAILY TEXAN

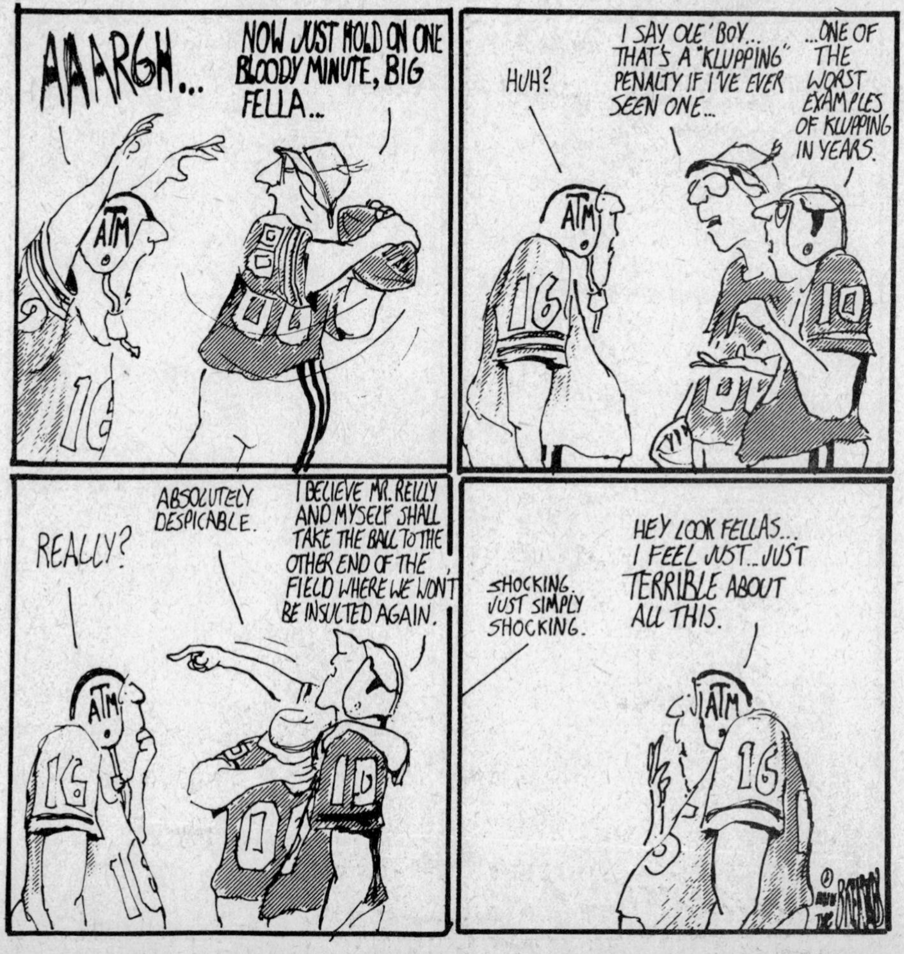
AAARGH...
NOW JUST HOLD ON ONE BLOODY MINUTE, BIG FELLA...
HUH?
I SAY OLE' BOY... THAT'S A "KLUPPING" PENALTY IF I'VE EVER SEEN ONE...
...ONE OF THE WORST EXAMPLES OF KLUPPING IN YEARS.
REALLY?
ABSOLUTELY DESPICABLE.
I BELIEVE MR. REILLY AND MYSELF SHALL TAKE THE BALL TO THE OTHER END OF THE FIELD WHERE WE WON'T BE INSULTED AGAIN.
SHOCKING. JUST SIMPLY SHOCKING.
HEY LOOK FELLAS... I FEEL JUST... JUST TERRIBLE ABOUT ALL THIS.

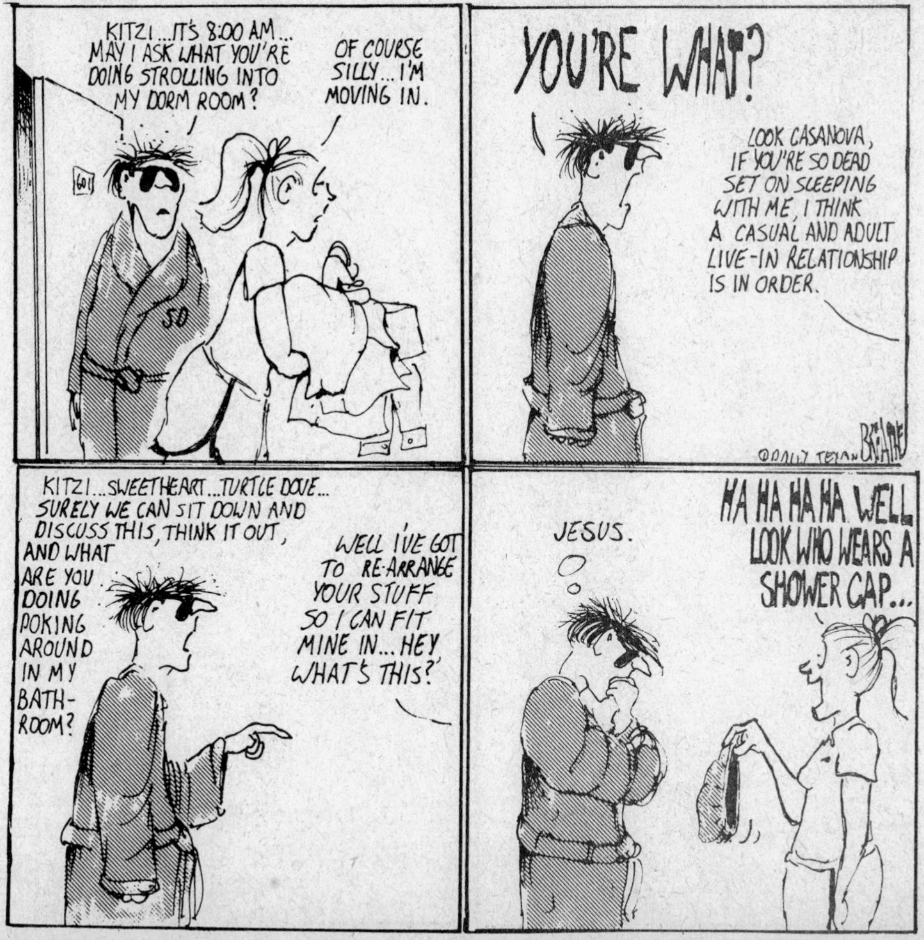
KITZI...IT'S 8:00 AM... MAY I ASK WHAT YOU'RE DOING STROLLING INTO MY DORM ROOM?
OF COURSE SILLY... I'M MOVING IN.
601
SO
YOU'RE WHAT?
LOOK CASANOVA, IF YOU'RE SO DEAD SET ON SLEEPING WITH ME, I THINK A CASUAL AND ADULT LIVE-IN RELATIONSHIP IS IN ORDER.
©DAILY TEXAN
BREATHED
KITZI...SWEETHEART...TURTLE DOVE... SURELY WE CAN SIT DOWN AND DISCUSS THIS, THINK IT OUT, AND WHAT ARE YOU DOING POKING AROUND IN MY BATH-ROOM?
WELL I'VE GOT TO RE-ARRANGE YOUR STUFF SO I CAN FIT MINE IN... HEY WHAT'S THIS?
JESUS.
HA HA HA HA WELL LOOK WHO WEARS A SHOWER CAP...

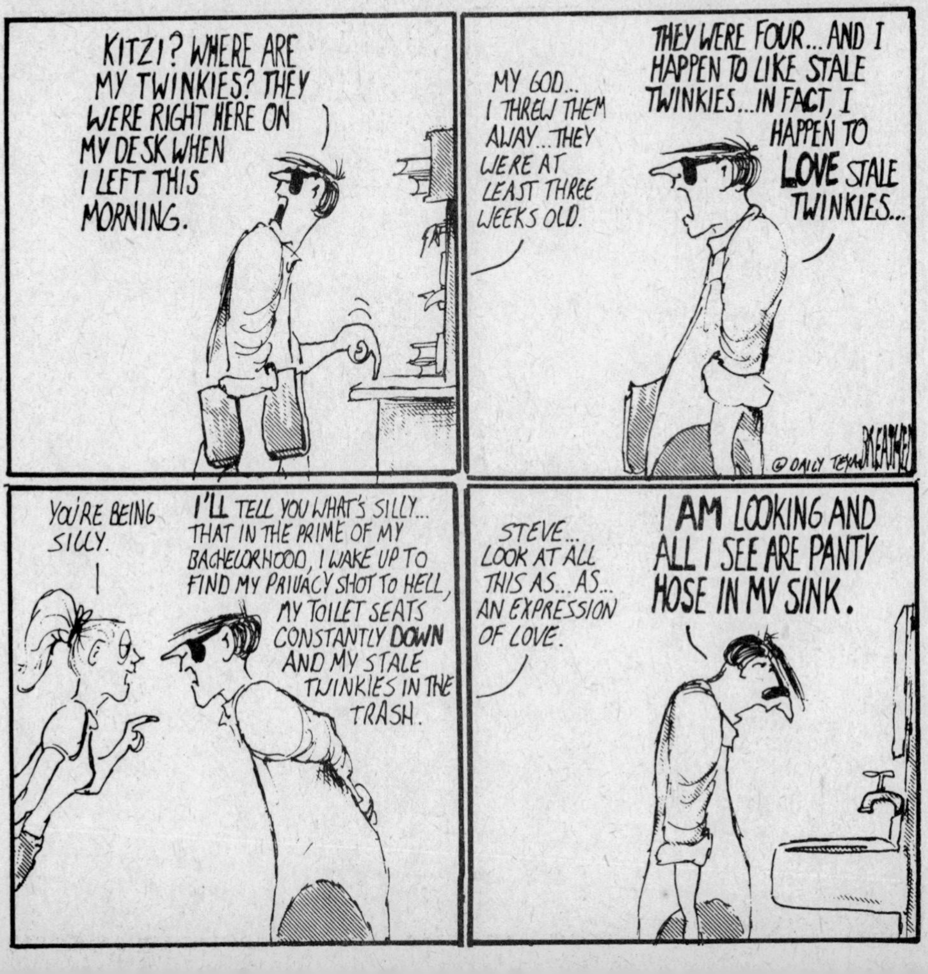
KITZI? WHERE ARE MY TWINKIES? THEY WERE RIGHT HERE ON MY DESK WHEN I LEFT THIS MORNING.
MY GOD... I THREW THEM AWAY...THEY WERE AT LEAST THREE WEEKS OLD.
THEY WERE FOUR... AND I HAPPEN TO LIKE STALE TWINKIES...IN FACT, I HAPPEN TO LOVE STALE TWINKIES...
© DAILY TEXAN
BREATHED
YOU'RE BEING SILLY.
I'LL TELL YOU WHAT'S SILLY... THAT IN THE PRIME OF MY BACHELORHOOD, I WAKE UP TO FIND MY PRIVACY SHOT TO HELL, MY TOILET SEATS CONSTANTLY DOWN AND MY STALE TWINKIES IN THE TRASH.
STEVE... LOOK AT ALL THIS AS...AS... AN EXPRESSION OF LOVE.
I AM LOOKING AND ALL I SEE ARE PANTY HOSE IN MY SINK.

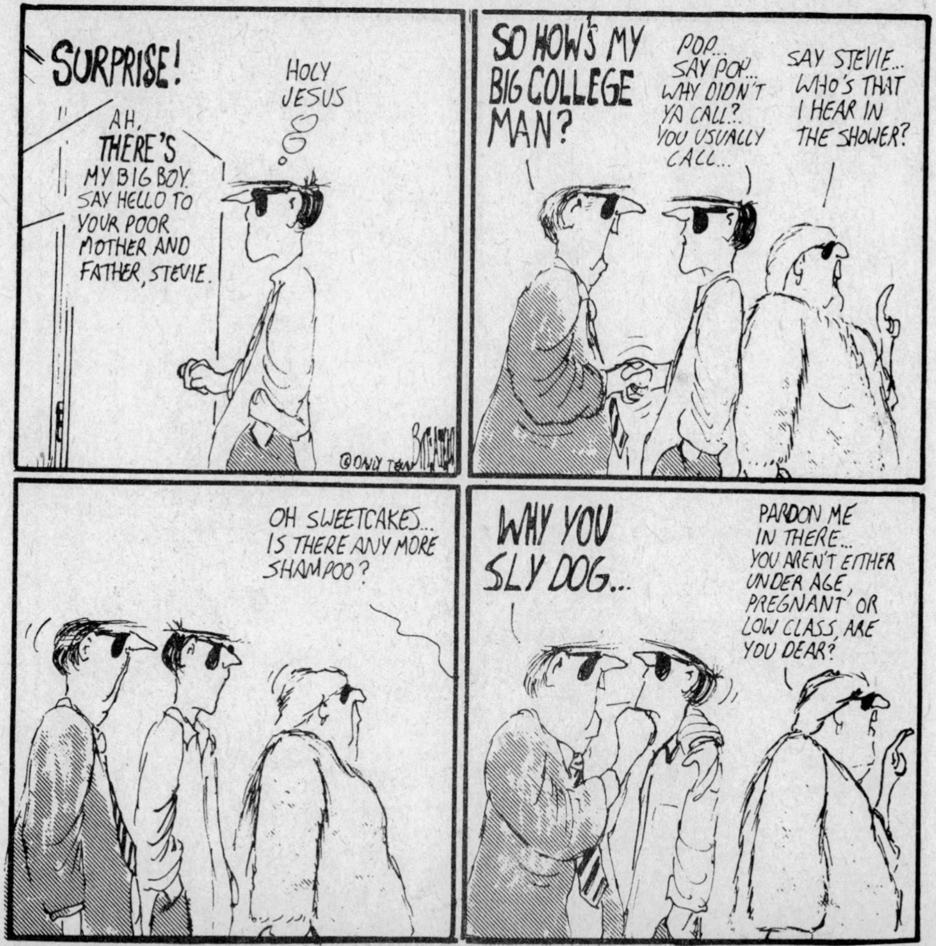
SURPRISE!
AH, THERE'S MY BIG BOY. SAY HELLO TO YOUR POOR MOTHER AND FATHER, STEVIE.
HOLY JESUS
SO HOW'S MY BIG COLLEGE MAN?
POP... SAY POP... WHY DIDN'T YA CALL?.. YOU USUALLY CALL...
SAY STEVIE... WHO'S THAT I HEAR IN THE SHOWER?
OH SWEETCAKES... IS THERE ANY MORE SHAMPOO?
WHY YOU SLY DOG...
PARDON ME IN THERE... YOU AREN'T EITHER UNDER AGE, PREGNANT OR LOW CLASS, ARE YOU DEAR?

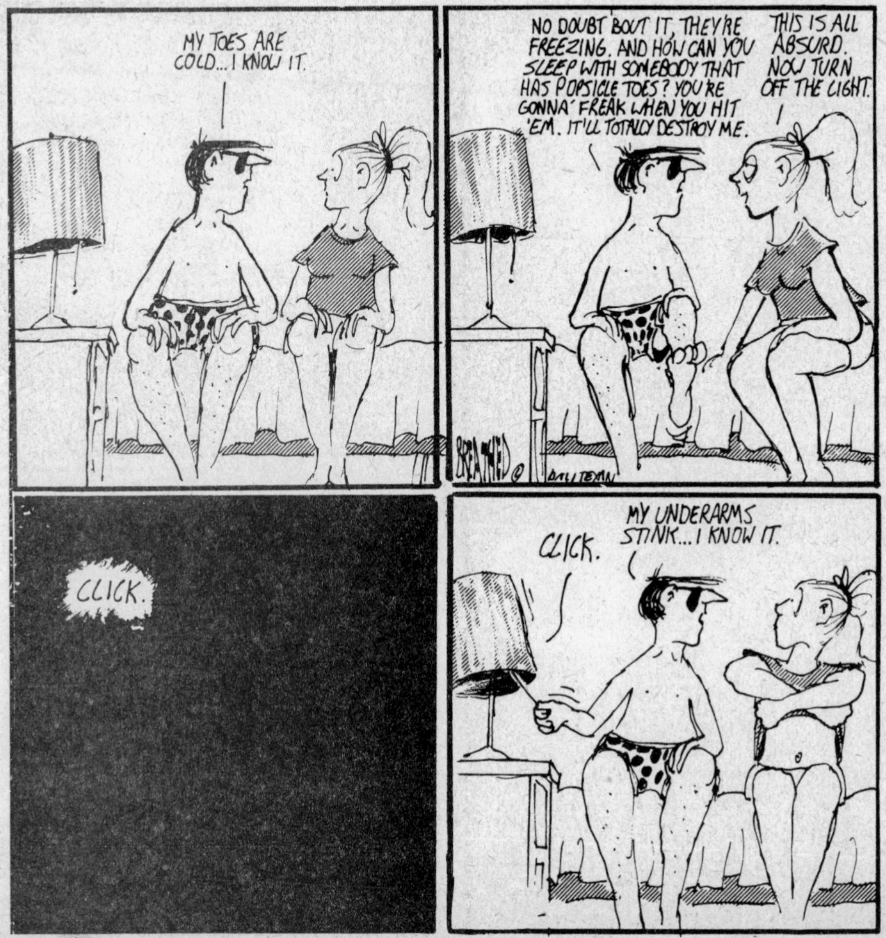
MY TOES ARE COLD... I KNOW IT.
NO DOUBT BOUT IT, THEY'RE FREEZING. AND HOW CAN YOU SLEEP WITH SOMEBODY THAT HAS POPSICLE TOES? YOU'RE GONNA' FREAK WHEN YOU HIT 'EM. IT'LL TOTALLY DESTROY ME.
THIS IS ALL ABSURD. NOW TURN OFF THE LIGHT.
BREATHED ©
CLICK.
CLICK.
MY UNDERARMS STINK... I KNOW IT.

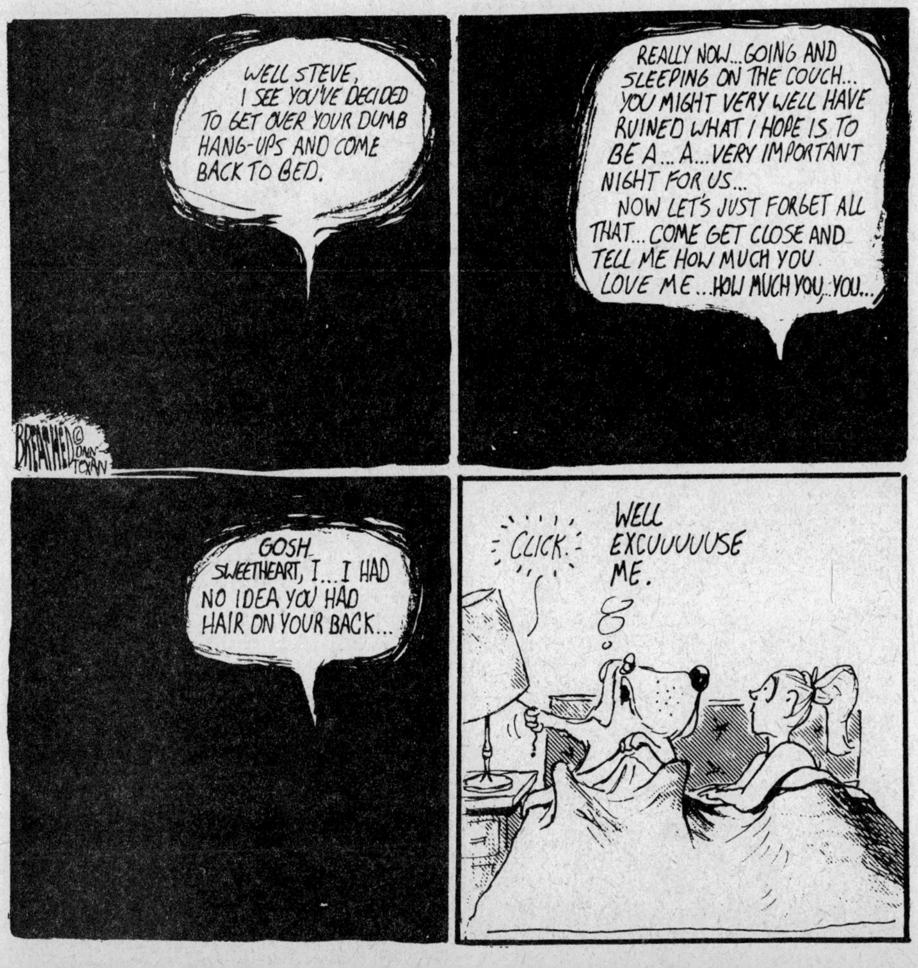
WELL STEVE, I SEE YOU'VE DECIDED TO GET OVER YOUR DUMB HANG-UPS AND COME BACK TO BED.
REALLY NOW...GOING AND SLEEPING ON THE COUCH... YOU MIGHT VERY WELL HAVE RUINED WHAT I HOPE IS TO BE A... A...VERY IMPORTANT NIGHT FOR US... NOW LET'S JUST FORGET ALL THAT... COME GET CLOSE AND TELL ME HOW MUCH YOU LOVE ME...HOW MUCH YOU,..YOU...
BREATHED©
GOSH SWEETHEART, I...I HAD NO IDEA YOU HAD HAIR ON YOUR BACK...
CLICK
WELL EXCUUUUUSE ME.

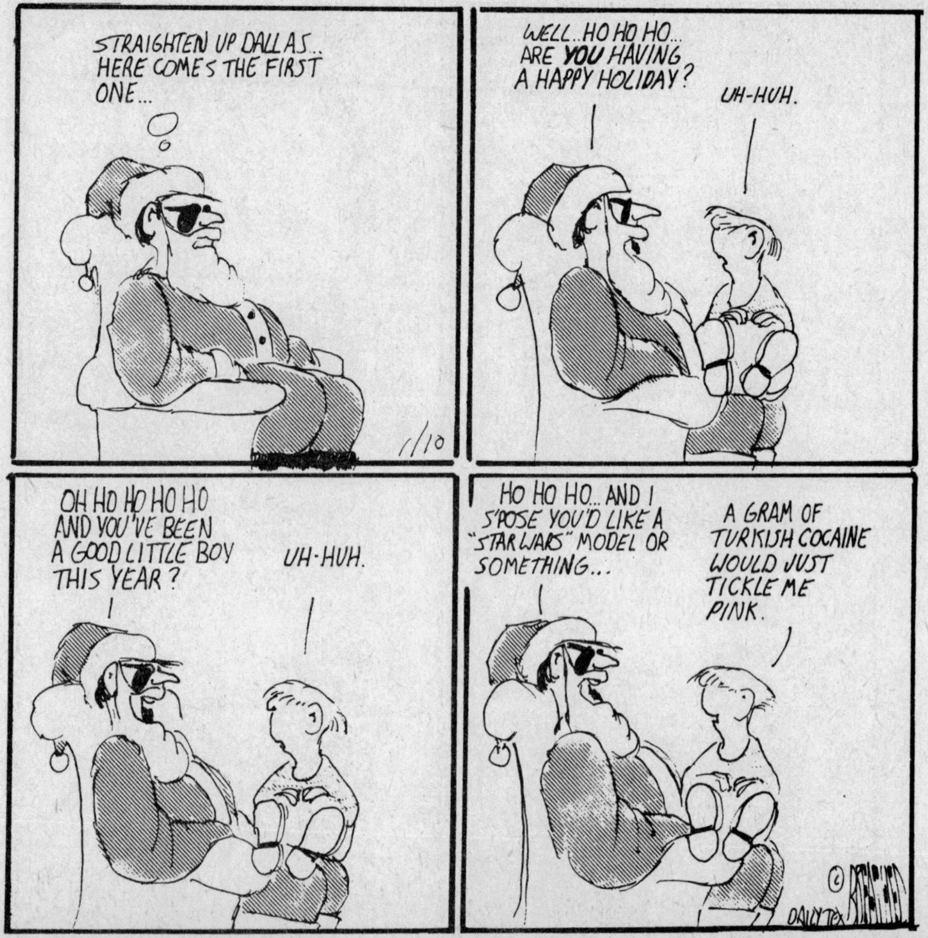
STRAIGHTEN UP DALLAS... HERE COMES THE FIRST ONE...
1/10
WELL...HO HO HO... ARE **YOU** HAVING A HAPPY HOLIDAY?
UH-HUH.
OH HO HO HO HO AND YOU'VE BEEN A GOOD LITTLE BOY THIS YEAR?
UH-HUH.
HO HO HO... AND I S'POSE YOU'D LIKE A "STAR WARS" MODEL OR SOMETHING...
A GRAM OF TURKISH COCAINE WOULD JUST TICKLE ME PINK.

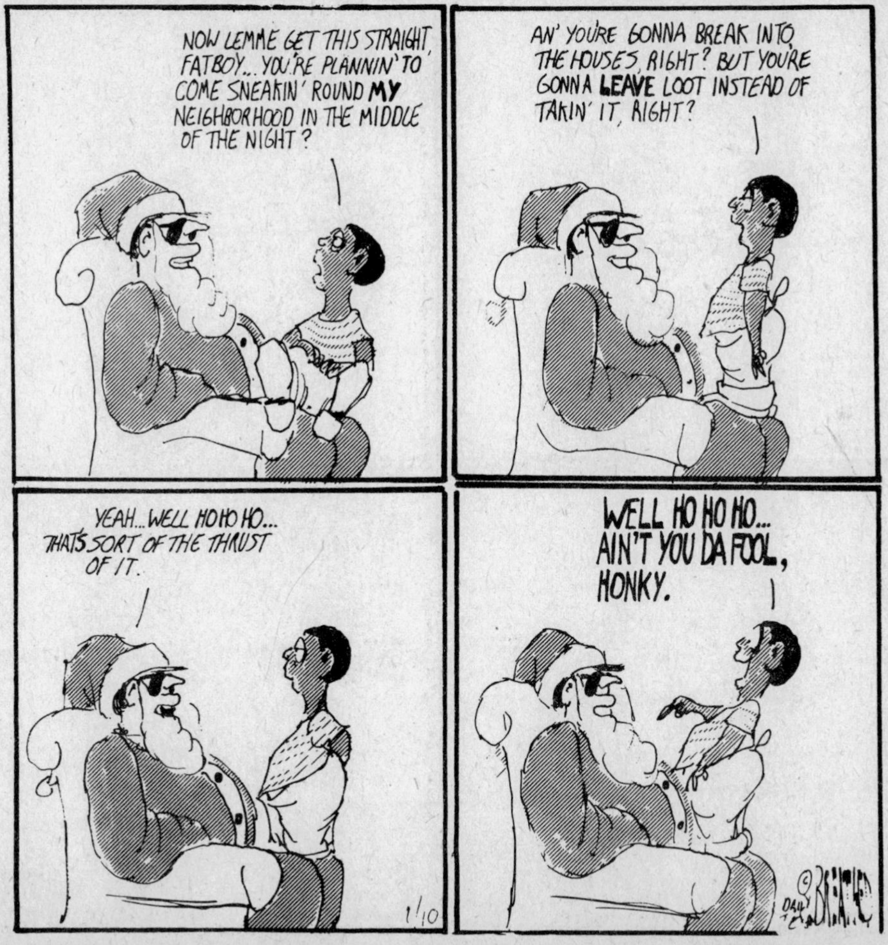
NOW LEMME GET THIS STRAIGHT, FATBOY... YOU'RE PLANNIN' TO COME SNEAKIN' ROUND **MY** NEIGHBORHOOD IN THE MIDDLE OF THE NIGHT?
AN' YOU'RE GONNA BREAK INTO THE HOUSES, RIGHT? BUT YOU'RE GONNA **LEAVE** LOOT INSTEAD OF TAKIN' IT, RIGHT?
YEAH... WELL HO HO HO... THAT'S SORT OF THE THRUST OF IT.
1/10
WELL HO HO HO... AIN'T YOU DA FOOL, HONKY.

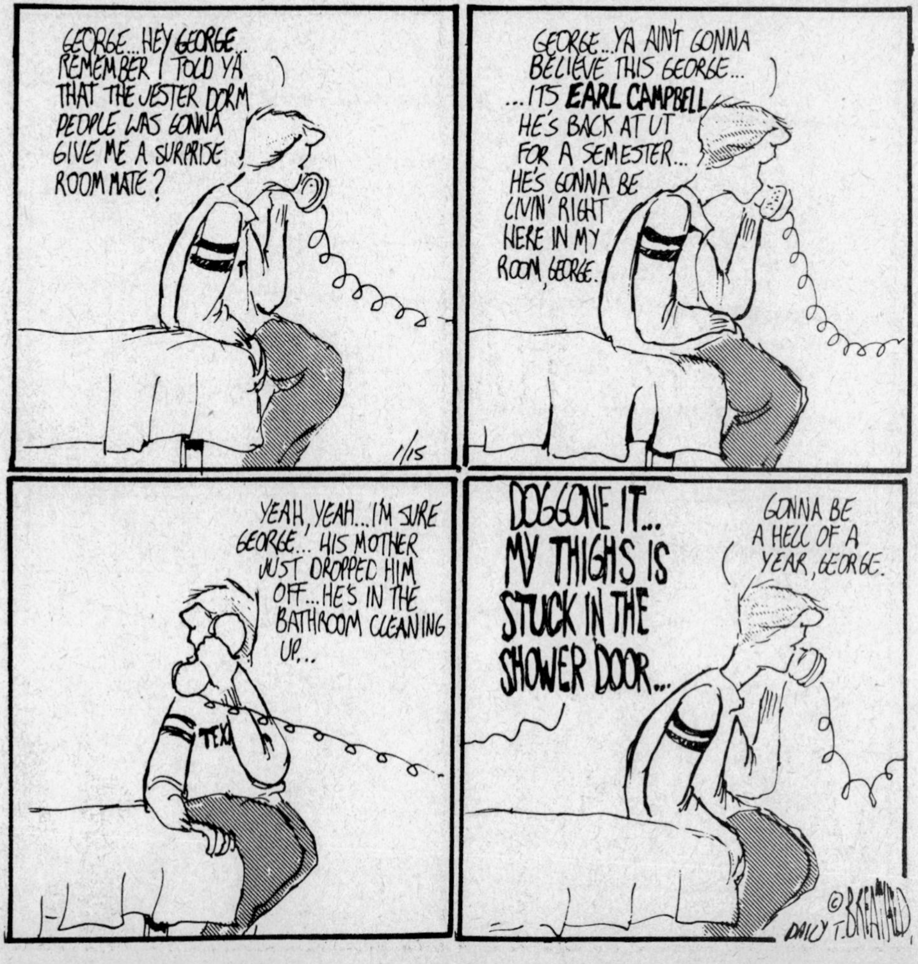
GEORGE... HEY GEORGE... REMEMBER I TOLD YA THAT THE JESTER DORM PEOPLE WAS GONNA GIVE ME A SURPRISE ROOMMATE?
1/15
GEORGE... YA AIN'T GONNA BELIEVE THIS GEORGE... ...ITS EARL CAMPBELL HE'S BACK AT UT FOR A SEMESTER... HE'S GONNA BE LIVIN' RIGHT HERE IN MY ROOM, GEORGE.
YEAH, YEAH... I'M SURE GEORGE... HIS MOTHER JUST DROPPED HIM OFF... HE'S IN THE BATHROOM CLEANING UP...
TEX
DOGGONE IT... MY THIGHS IS STUCK IN THE SHOWER DOOR...
GONNA BE A HELL OF A YEAR, GEORGE.
© DAILY T. BREATHED

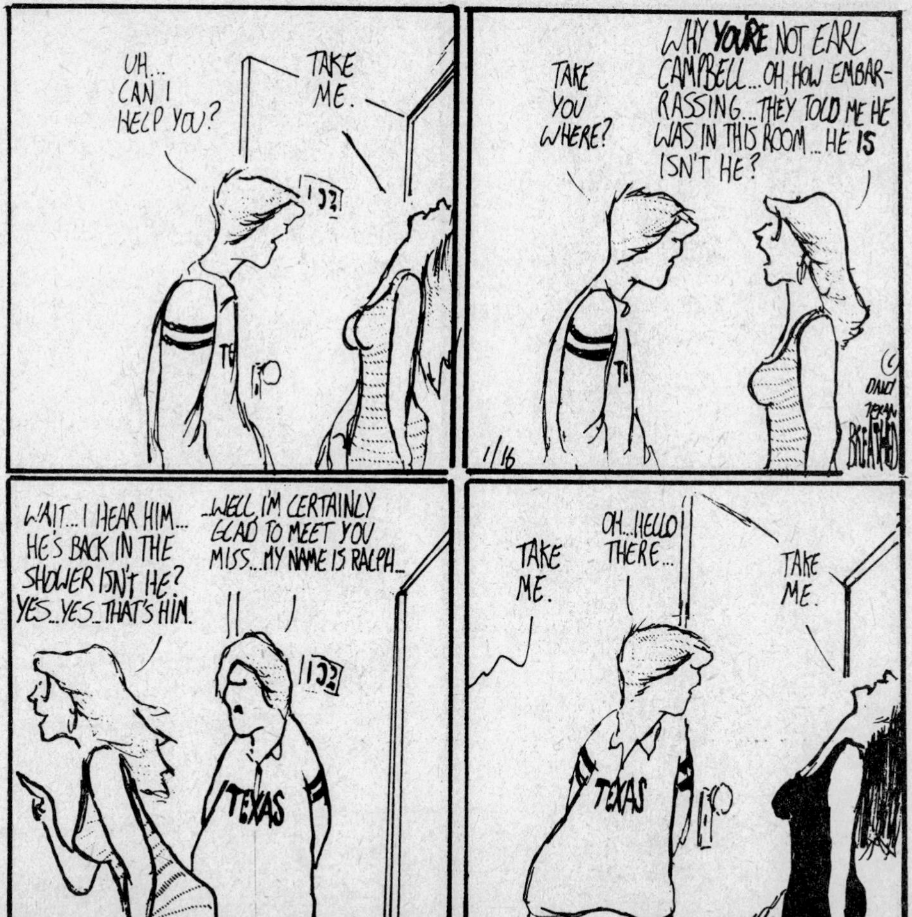
UH... CAN I HELP YOU?
TAKE ME.
TAKE YOU WHERE?
WHY YOU'RE NOT EARL CAMPBELL...OH, HOW EMBARRASSING...THEY TOLD ME HE WAS IN THIS ROOM...HE IS ISN'T HE?
1/16
WAIT...I HEAR HIM... HE'S BACK IN THE SHOWER ISN'T HE? YES...YES...THAT'S HIM.
...WELL, I'M CERTAINLY GLAD TO MEET YOU MISS...MY NAME IS RALPH...
TEXAS
TAKE ME.
OH...HELLO THERE...
TAKE ME.
TEXAS

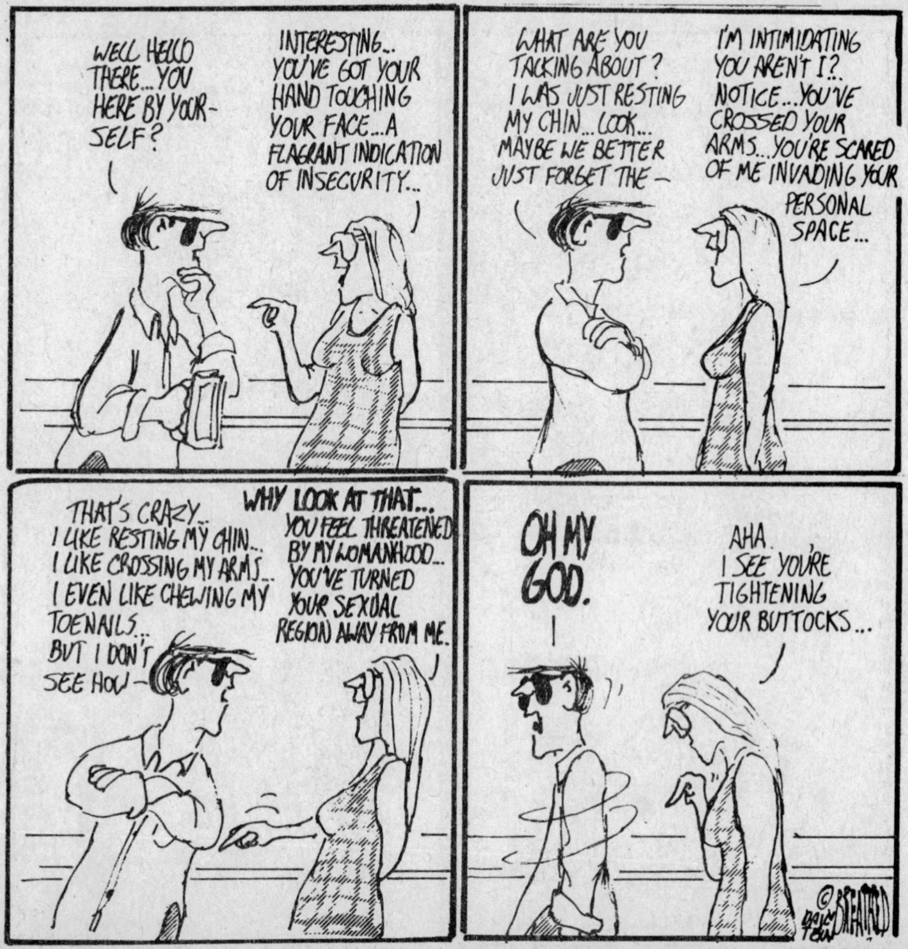
WELL HELLO THERE... YOU HERE BY YOURSELF?
INTERESTING... YOU'VE GOT YOUR HAND TOUCHING YOUR FACE... A FLAGRANT INDICATION OF INSECURITY...
WHAT ARE YOU TALKING ABOUT? I WAS JUST RESTING MY CHIN... LOOK... MAYBE WE BETTER JUST FORGET THE—
I'M INTIMIDATING YOU AREN'T I?.. NOTICE... YOU'VE CROSSED YOUR ARMS... YOU'RE SCARED OF ME INVADING YOUR PERSONAL SPACE...
THAT'S CRAZY... I LIKE RESTING MY CHIN... I LIKE CROSSING MY ARMS... I EVEN LIKE CHEWING MY TOENAILS... BUT I DON'T SEE HOW—
WHY LOOK AT THAT... YOU FEEL THREATENED BY MY WOMANHOOD... YOU'VE TURNED YOUR SEXUAL REGION AWAY FROM ME.
OH MY GOD.
AHA. I SEE YOU'RE TIGHTENING YOUR BUTTOCKS...
© BREATHED

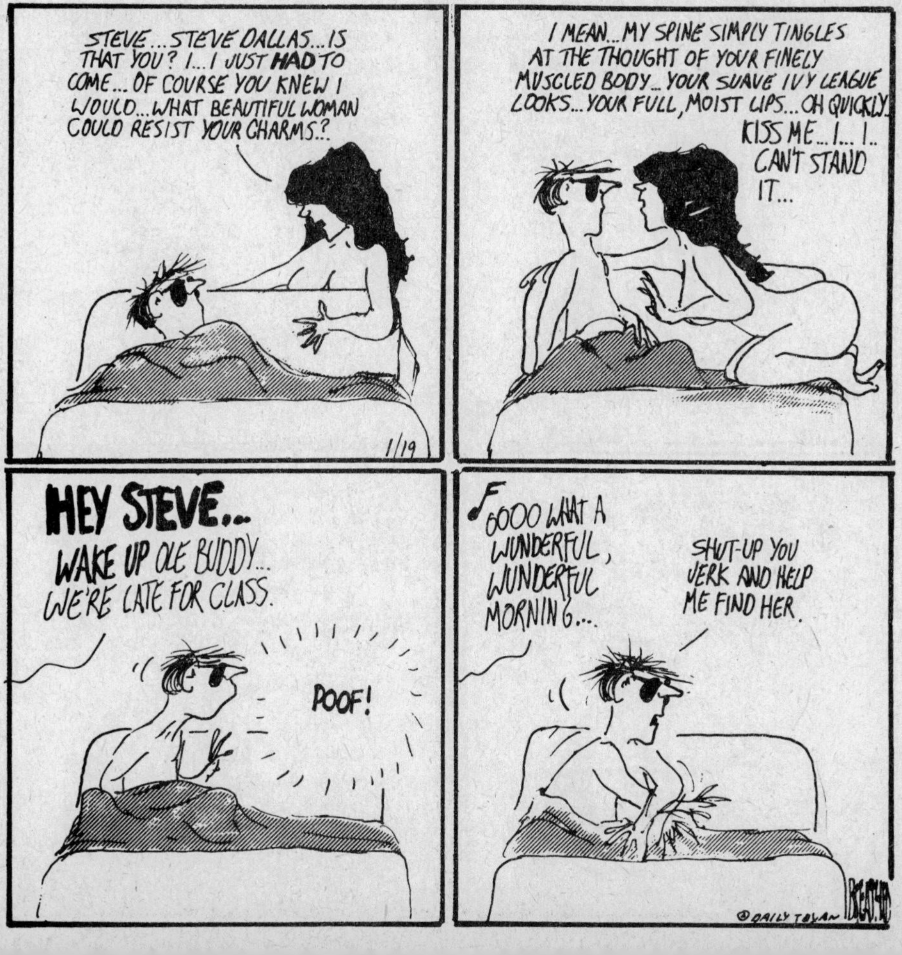
STEVE... STEVE DALLAS... IS THAT YOU? I... I JUST HAD TO COME... OF COURSE YOU KNEW I WOULD... WHAT BEAUTIFUL WOMAN COULD RESIST YOUR CHARMS.?
1/19
I MEAN... MY SPINE SIMPLY TINGLES AT THE THOUGHT OF YOUR FINELY MUSCLED BODY... YOUR SUAVE IVY LEAGUE LOOKS... YOUR FULL, MOIST LIPS... OH QUICKLY
KISS ME... I... I.. CAN'T STAND IT...
HEY STEVE...
WAKE UP OLE BUDDY... WE'RE LATE FOR CLASS.
POOF!
OOOO WHAT A WUNDERFUL, WUNDERFUL MORNING...
SHUT-UP YOU JERK AND HELP ME FIND HER.
© DAILY TEXAN
BREATHED

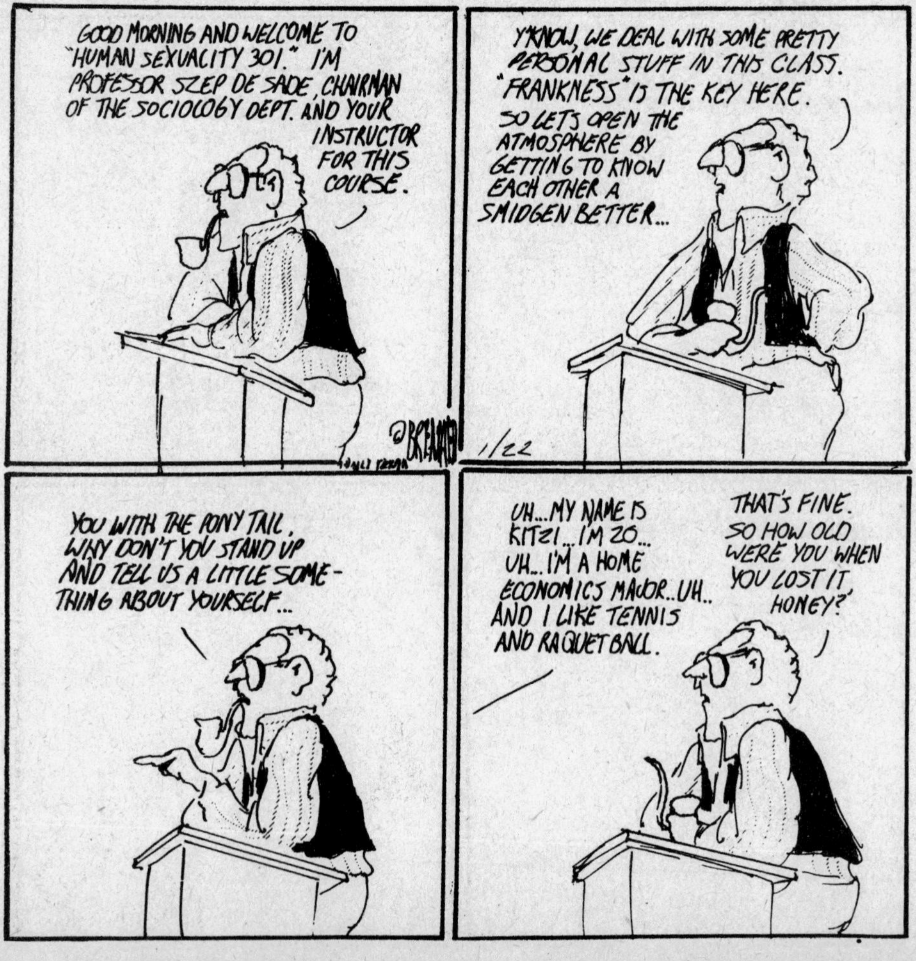
GOOD MORNING AND WELCOME TO "HUMAN SEXUALITY 301." I'M PROFESSOR SZEP DE SADE, CHAIRMAN OF THE SOCIOLOGY DEPT. AND YOUR INSTRUCTOR FOR THIS COURSE.
©BREATHED
1/22
Y'KNOW, WE DEAL WITH SOME PRETTY PERSONAL STUFF IN THIS CLASS. "FRANKNESS" IS THE KEY HERE.
SO LET'S OPEN THE ATMOSPHERE BY GETTING TO KNOW EACH OTHER A SMIDGEN BETTER...
YOU WITH THE PONY TAIL, WHY DON'T YOU STAND UP AND TELL US A LITTLE SOME-THING ABOUT YOURSELF...
UH...MY NAME IS KITZI...I'M 20... UH...I'M A HOME ECONOMICS MAJOR..UH.. AND I LIKE TENNIS AND RAQUETBALL.
THAT'S FINE. SO HOW OLD WERE YOU WHEN YOU LOST IT, HONEY?

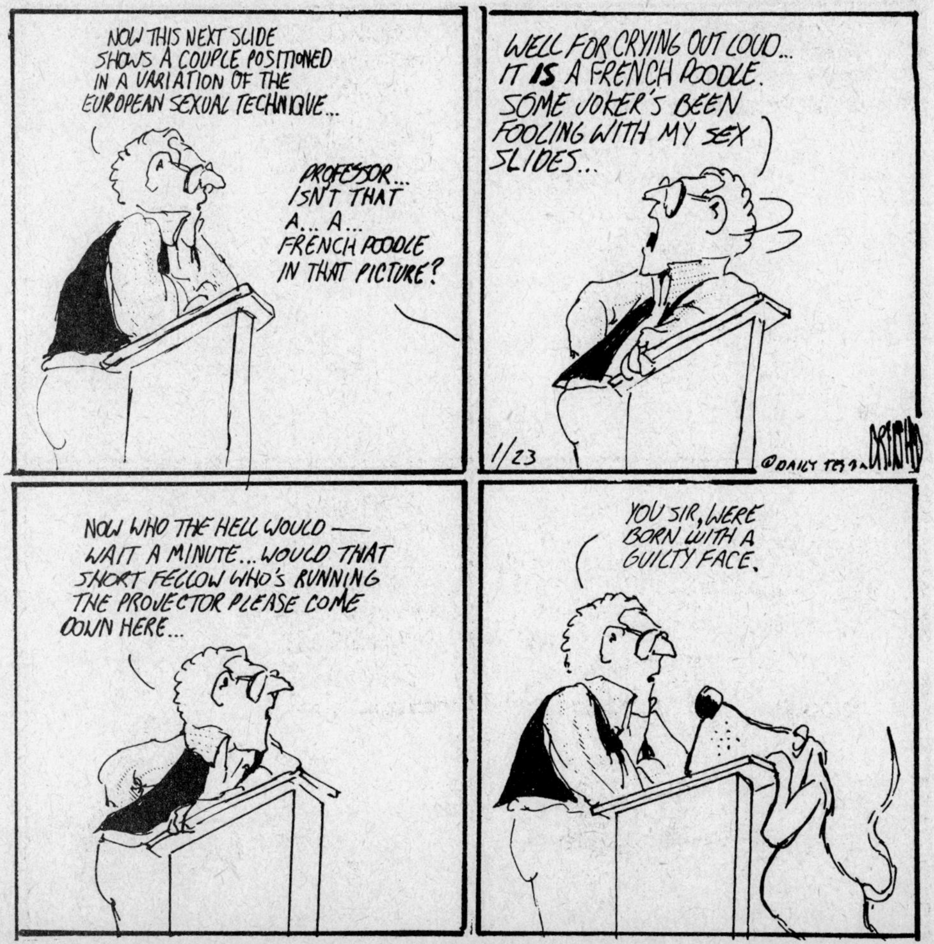
NOW THIS NEXT SLIDE SHOWS A COUPLE POSITIONED IN A VARIATION OF THE EUROPEAN SEXUAL TECHNIQUE...
PROFESSOR... ISN'T THAT A... A... FRENCH POODLE IN THAT PICTURE?
WELL FOR CRYING OUT LOUD... IT IS A FRENCH POODLE. SOME JOKER'S BEEN FOOLING WITH MY SEX SLIDES...
1/23
©DAILY TEXAN
NOW WHO THE HELL WOULD — WAIT A MINUTE... WOULD THAT SHORT FELLOW WHO'S RUNNING THE PROJECTOR PLEASE COME DOWN HERE...
YOU SIR, WERE BORN WITH A GUILTY FACE.

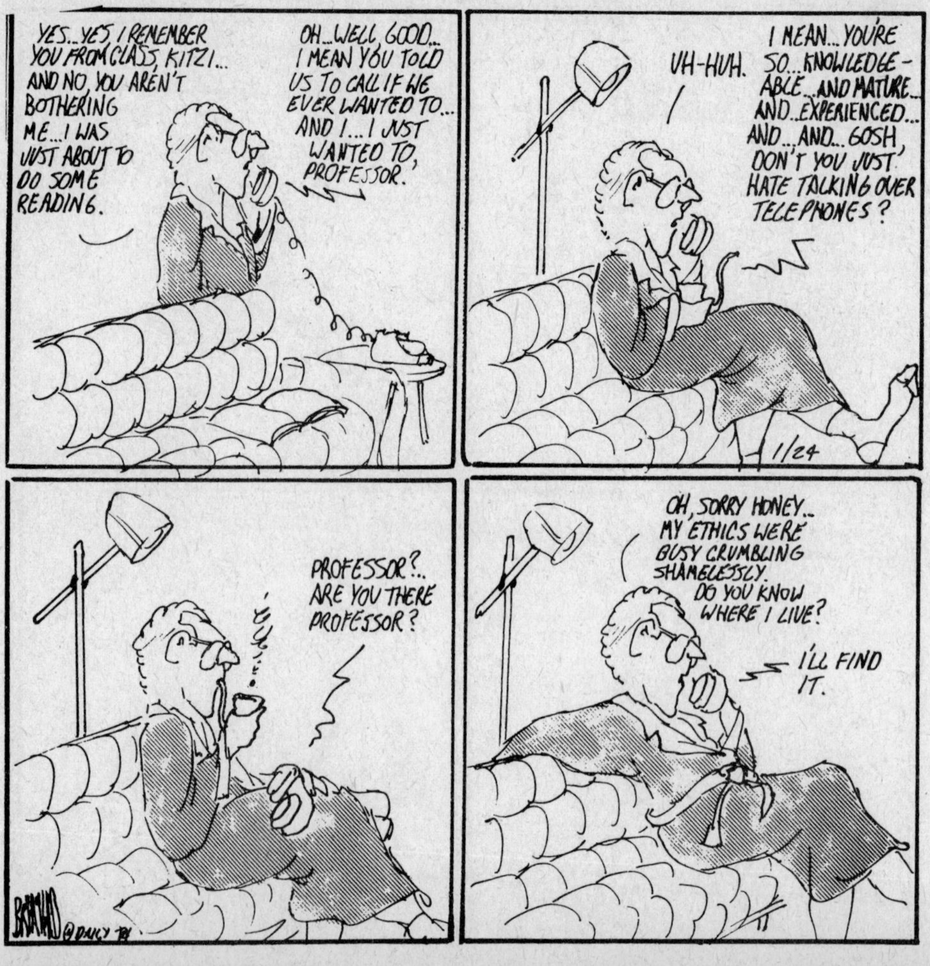
YES...YES, I REMEMBER YOU FROM CLASS, KITZI... AND NO, YOU AREN'T BOTHERING ME...I WAS JUST ABOUT TO DO SOME READING.
OH...WELL, GOOD... I MEAN YOU TOLD US TO CALL IF WE EVER WANTED TO... AND I... I JUST WANTED TO, PROFESSOR.
UH-HUH.
I MEAN... YOU'RE SO... KNOWLEDGE-ABLE...AND MATURE... AND..EXPERIENCED... AND...AND... GOSH, DON'T YOU JUST HATE TALKING OVER TELEPHONES?
1/24
PROFESSOR?... ARE YOU THERE PROFESSOR?
OH, SORRY HONEY... MY ETHICS WERE BUSY CRUMBLING SHAMELESSLY. DO YOU KNOW WHERE I LIVE?
I'LL FIND IT.

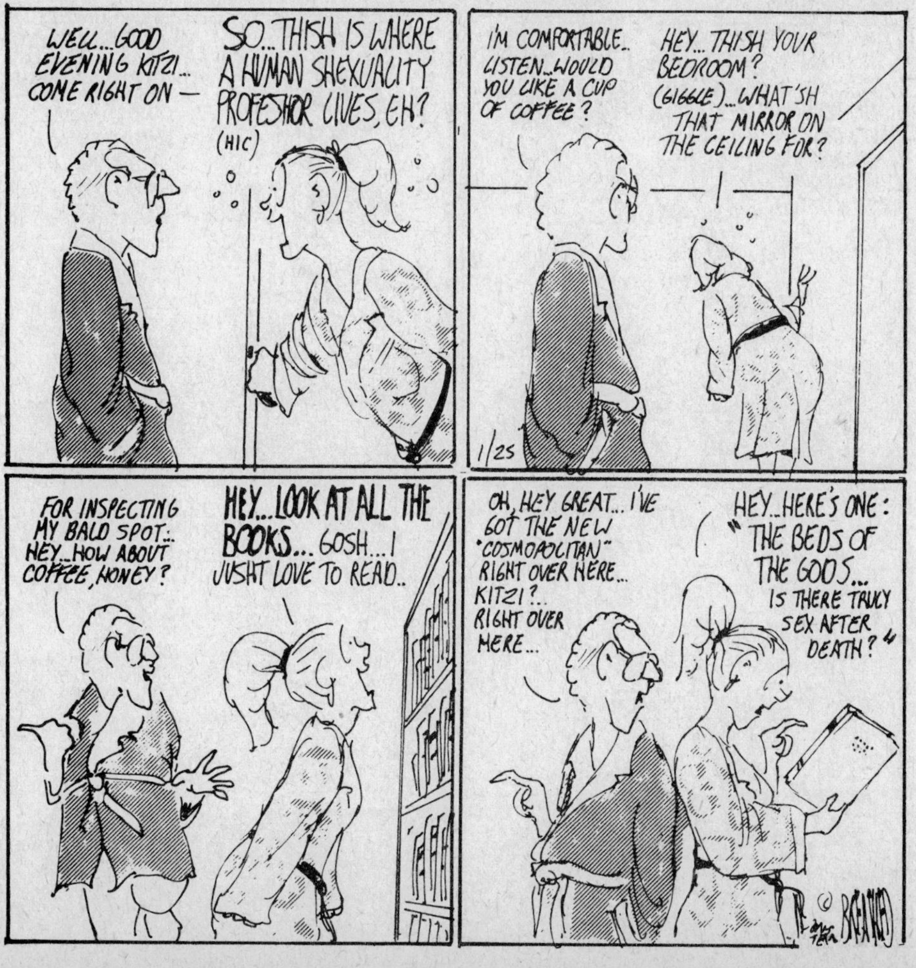
WELL...GOOD EVENING KITZI... COME RIGHT ON —
SO...THISH IS WHERE A HUMAN SHEXUALITY PROFESHOR LIVES, EH? (HIC)
I'M COMFORTABLE.. LISTEN..WOULD YOU LIKE A CUP OF COFFEE?
HEY... THISH YOUR BEDROOM? (GIGGLE)...WHAT'SH THAT MIRROR ON THE CEILING FOR?
1/25
FOR INSPECTING MY BALD SPOT.. HEY...HOW ABOUT COFFEE, HONEY?
HEY...LOOK AT ALL THE BOOKS... GOSH...I JUSHT LOVE TO READ..
OH, HEY GREAT... I'VE GOT THE NEW "COSMOPOLITAN" RIGHT OVER HERE... KITZI?.. RIGHT OVER HERE...
HEY..HERE'S ONE: "THE BEDS OF THE GODS... IS THERE TRULY SEX AFTER DEATH?"

AH...YONDER MORNING SUN AWAKENS THE SWEET SOUNDS OF THE NEW DAY.
OH MY GOD...WHAT AM I DOING HERE?
OH GEE...IT MUST HAVE BEEN THE ALCOHOL.
OH GOSH...IT WAS THE ALCOHOL...OH GOSH.
I FEEL SO... SO...CHEAP.
OH MY...I FEEL SO... SO...CHEAP...SO WANTON. (SOB..)
WELL THEN... GOT IT ALL OUT OF YOUR SYSTEM, HONEY?
YEAH. OH HEY, HOW DO YOU LIKE YOUR EGGS?
BREATHED

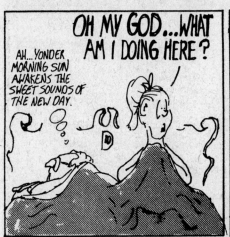

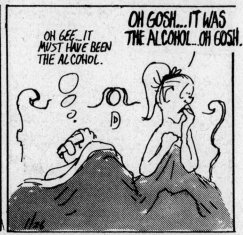

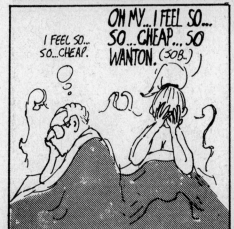

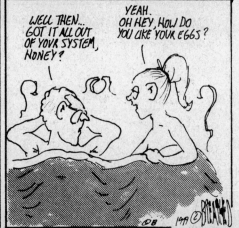

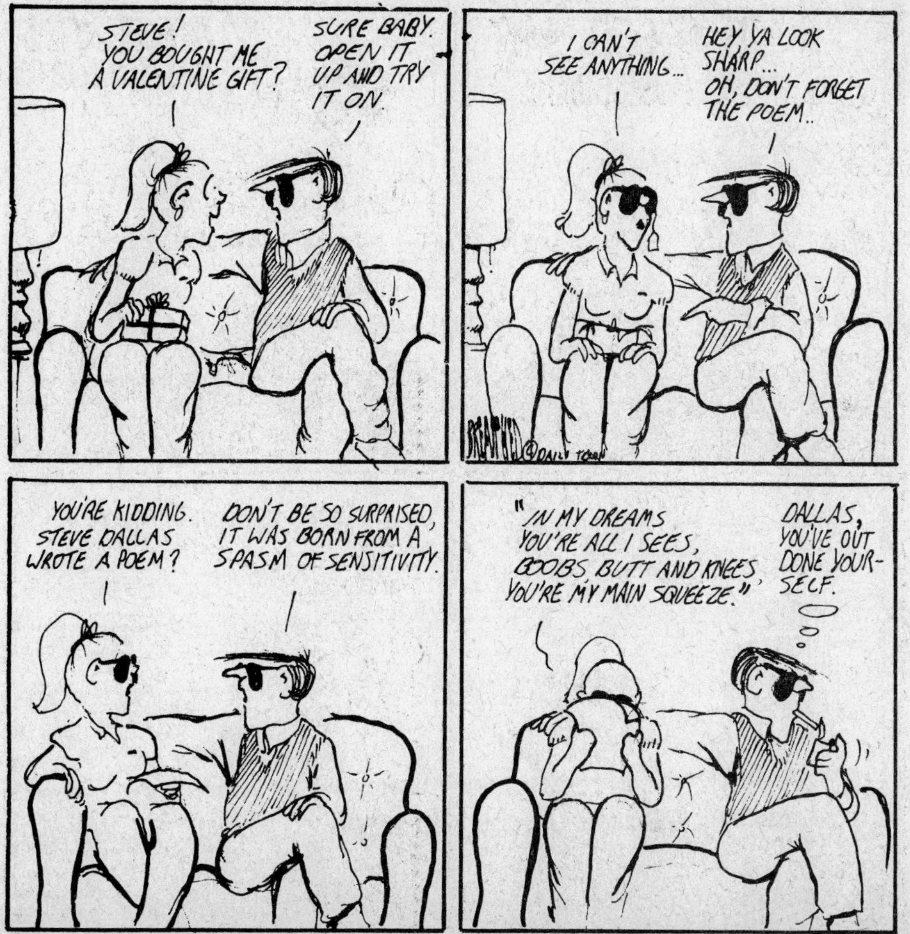
STEVE! YOU BOUGHT ME A VALENTINE GIFT?
SURE BABY. OPEN IT UP AND TRY IT ON.
I CAN'T SEE ANYTHING...
HEY YA LOOK SHARP... OH, DON'T FORGET THE POEM..
YOU'RE KIDDING. STEVE DALLAS WROTE A POEM?
DON'T BE SO SURPRISED, IT WAS BORN FROM A SPASM OF SENSITIVITY.
"IN MY DREAMS YOU'RE ALL I SEES, BOOBS BUTT AND KNEES, YOU'RE MY MAIN SQUEEZE."
DALLAS, YOU'VE OUT DONE YOURSELF.

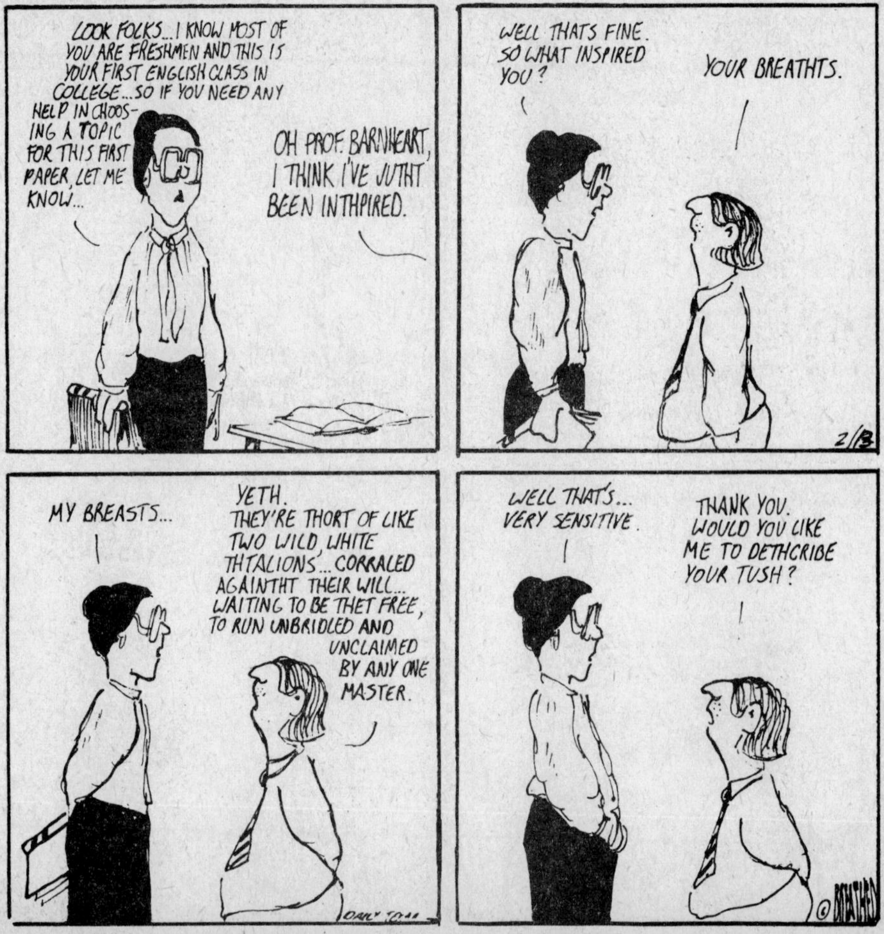
LOOK FOLKS... I KNOW MOST OF YOU ARE FRESHMEN AND THIS IS YOUR FIRST ENGLISH CLASS IN COLLEGE... SO IF YOU NEED ANY HELP IN CHOOSING A TOPIC FOR THIS FIRST PAPER, LET ME KNOW...
OH PROF. BARNHEART, I THINK I'VE JUTHT BEEN INTHPIRED.
WELL THATS FINE. SO WHAT INSPIRED YOU?
YOUR BREATHTS.
MY BREASTS...
YETH. THEY'RE THORT OF LIKE TWO WILD, WHITE THTALIONS... CORRALED AGAINTHT THEIR WILL... WAITING TO BE THET FREE, TO RUN UNBRIDLED AND UNCLAIMED BY ANY ONE MASTER.
WELL THAT'S... VERY SENSITIVE.
THANK YOU. WOULD YOU LIKE ME TO DETHCRIBE YOUR TUSH?

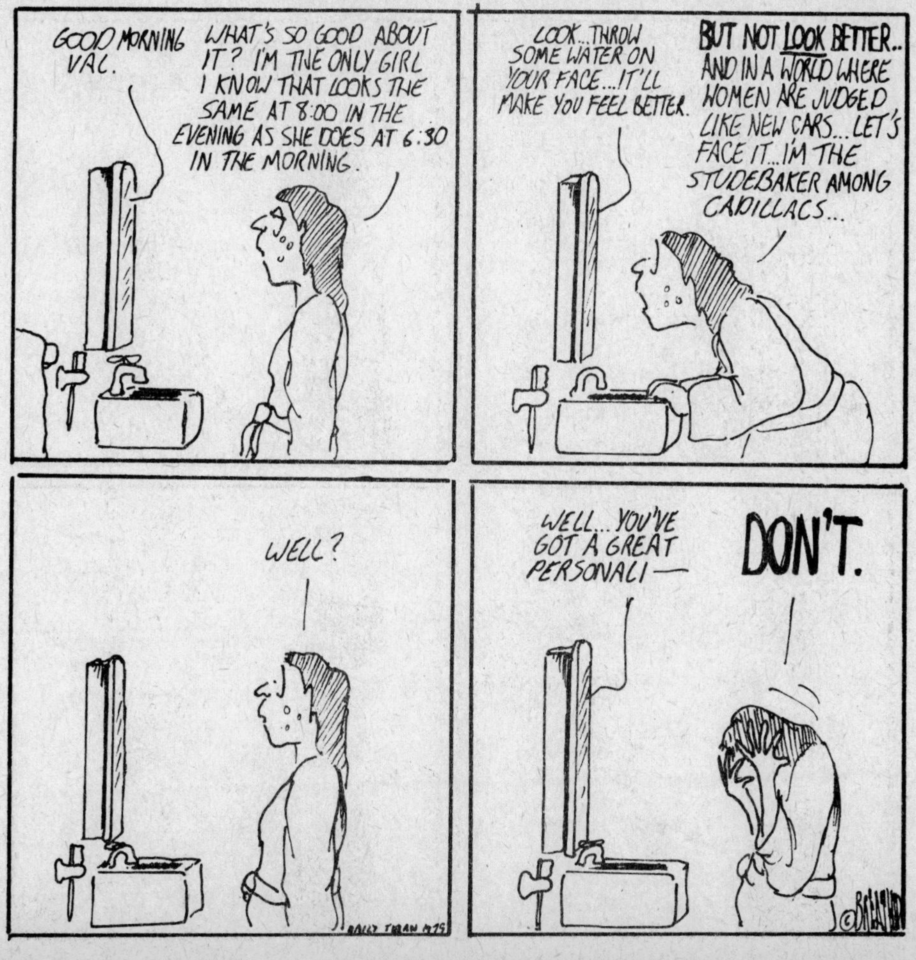
GOOD MORNING VAL.
WHAT'S SO GOOD ABOUT IT? I'M THE ONLY GIRL I KNOW THAT LOOKS THE SAME AT 8:00 IN THE EVENING AS SHE DOES AT 6:30 IN THE MORNING.
LOOK...THROW SOME WATER ON YOUR FACE...IT'LL MAKE YOU FEEL BETTER.
BUT NOT LOOK BETTER.. AND IN A WORLD WHERE WOMEN ARE JUDGED LIKE NEW CARS... LET'S FACE IT...I'M THE STUDEBAKER AMONG CADILLACS...
WELL?
WELL... YOU'VE GOT A GREAT PERSONALI—
DON'T.

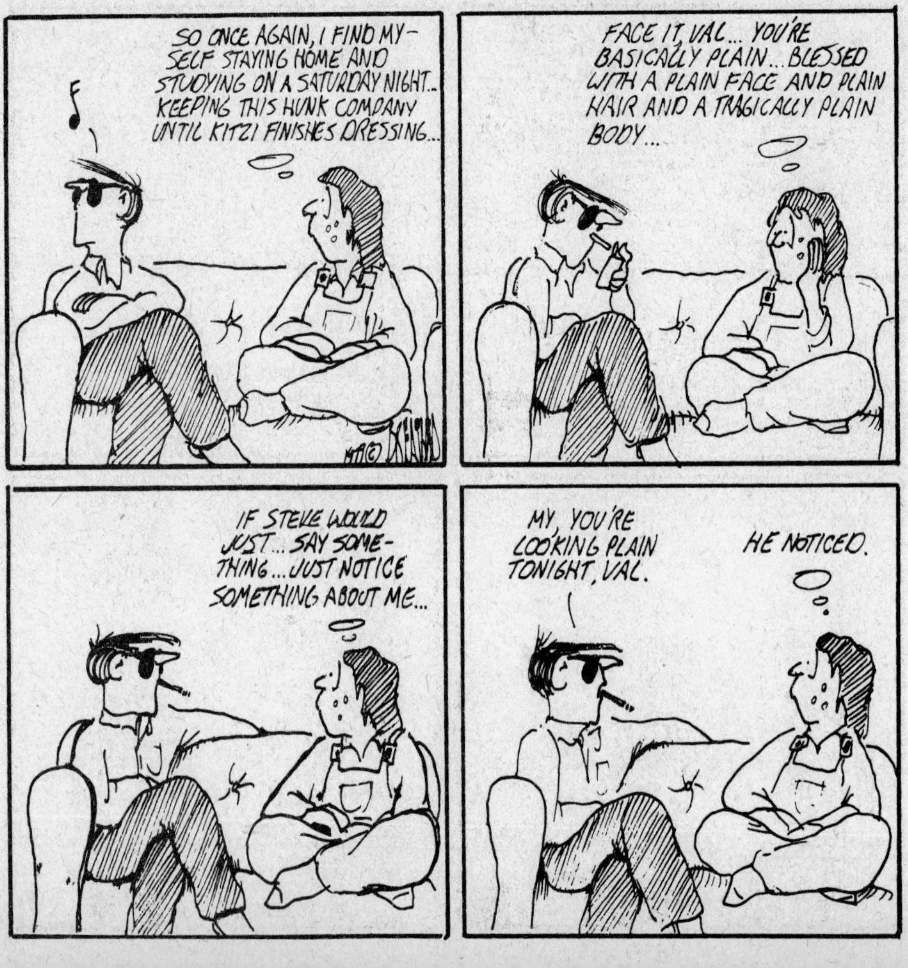
SO ONCE AGAIN, I FIND MYSELF STAYING HOME AND STUDYING ON A SATURDAY NIGHT.. KEEPING THIS HUNK COMPANY UNTIL KITZI FINISHES DRESSING...
FACE IT, VAL... YOU'RE BASICALLY PLAIN... BLESSED WITH A PLAIN FACE AND PLAIN HAIR AND A TRAGICALLY PLAIN BODY...
IF STEVE WOULD JUST... SAY SOMETHING... JUST NOTICE SOMETHING ABOUT ME...
MY, YOU'RE LOOKING PLAIN TONIGHT, VAL.
HE NOTICED.

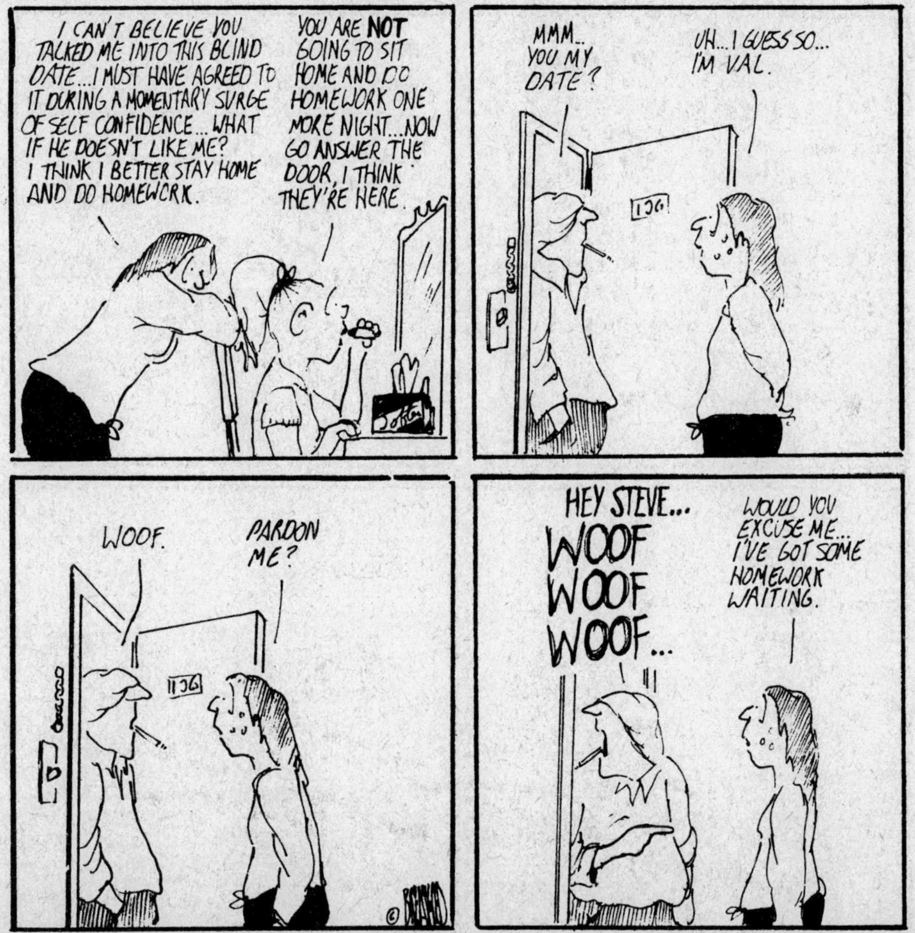
I CAN'T BELIEVE YOU TALKED ME INTO THIS BLIND DATE... I MUST HAVE AGREED TO IT DURING A MOMENTARY SURGE OF SELF CONFIDENCE... WHAT IF HE DOESN'T LIKE ME? I THINK I BETTER STAY HOME AND DO HOMEWORK.
YOU ARE **NOT** GOING TO SIT HOME AND DO HOMEWORK ONE MORE NIGHT... NOW GO ANSWER THE DOOR, I THINK THEY'RE HERE.
MMM.. YOU MY DATE?
UH... I GUESS SO... I'M VAL.
1136
WOOF.
PARDON ME?
1136
HEY STEVE... WOOF WOOF WOOF...
WOULD YOU EXCUSE ME... I'VE GOT SOME HOMEWORK WAITING.

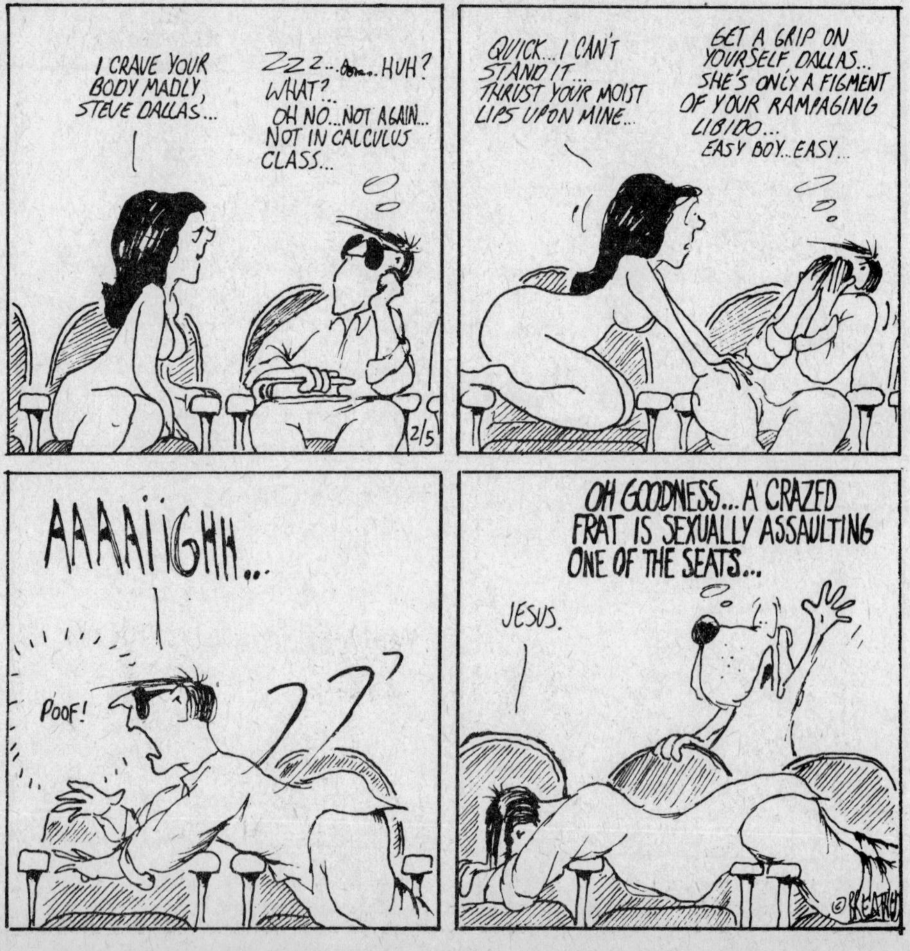
I CRAVE YOUR BODY MADLY, STEVE DALLAS...
ZZZ... HUH? WHAT?... OH NO...NOT AGAIN... NOT IN CALCULUS CLASS...
2/5
QUICK...I CAN'T STAND IT... THRUST YOUR MOIST LIPS UPON MINE...
GET A GRIP ON YOURSELF, DALLAS... SHE'S ONLY A FIGMENT OF YOUR RAMPAGING LIBIDO... EASY BOY...EASY...
AAAAIIGHH...
POOF!
OH GOODNESS...A CRAZED FRAT IS SEXUALLY ASSAULTING ONE OF THE SEATS...
JESUS.

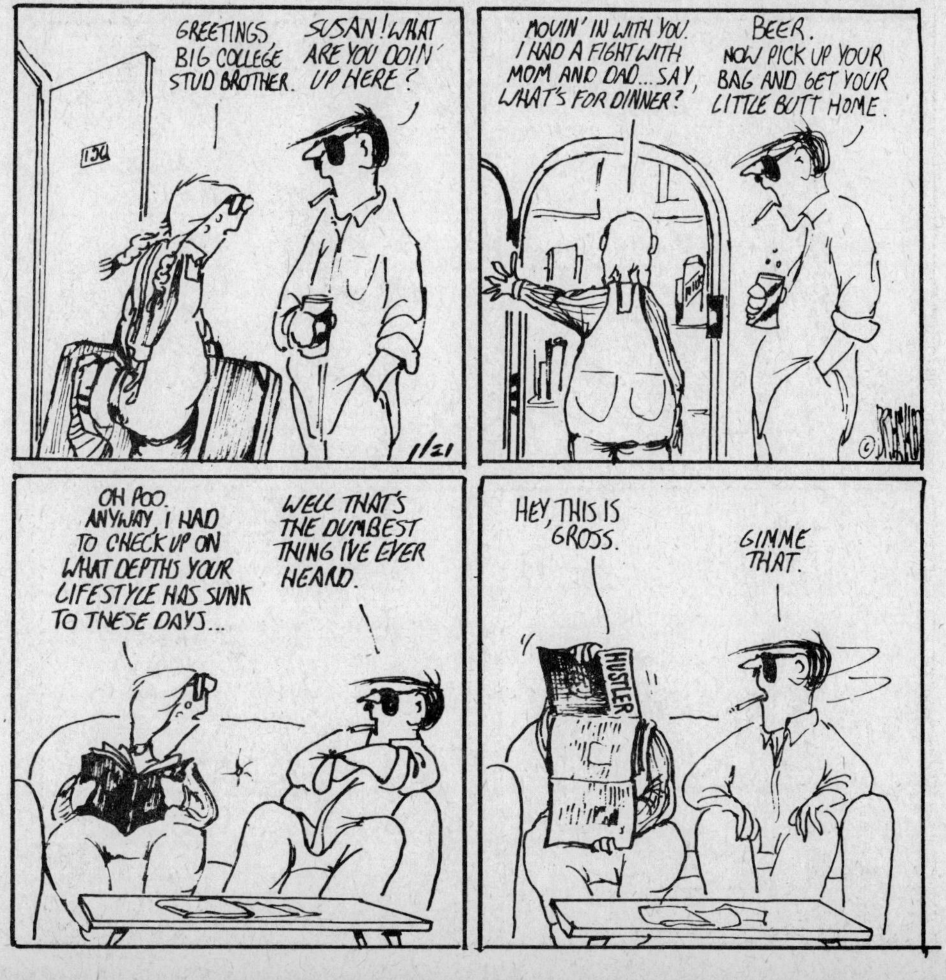
GREETINGS, BIG COLLEGE STUD BROTHER.
SUSAN! WHAT ARE YOU DOIN' UP HERE?
1/21
MOVIN' IN WITH YOU. I HAD A FIGHT WITH MOM AND DAD... SAY, WHAT'S FOR DINNER?
BEER. NOW PICK UP YOUR BAG AND GET YOUR LITTLE BUTT HOME.
OH POO. ANYWAY, I HAD TO CHECK UP ON WHAT DEPTHS YOUR LIFESTYLE HAS SUNK TO THESE DAYS...
WELL THAT'S THE DUMBEST THING IVE EVER HEARD.
HEY, THIS IS GROSS.
HUSTLER
GIMME THAT.

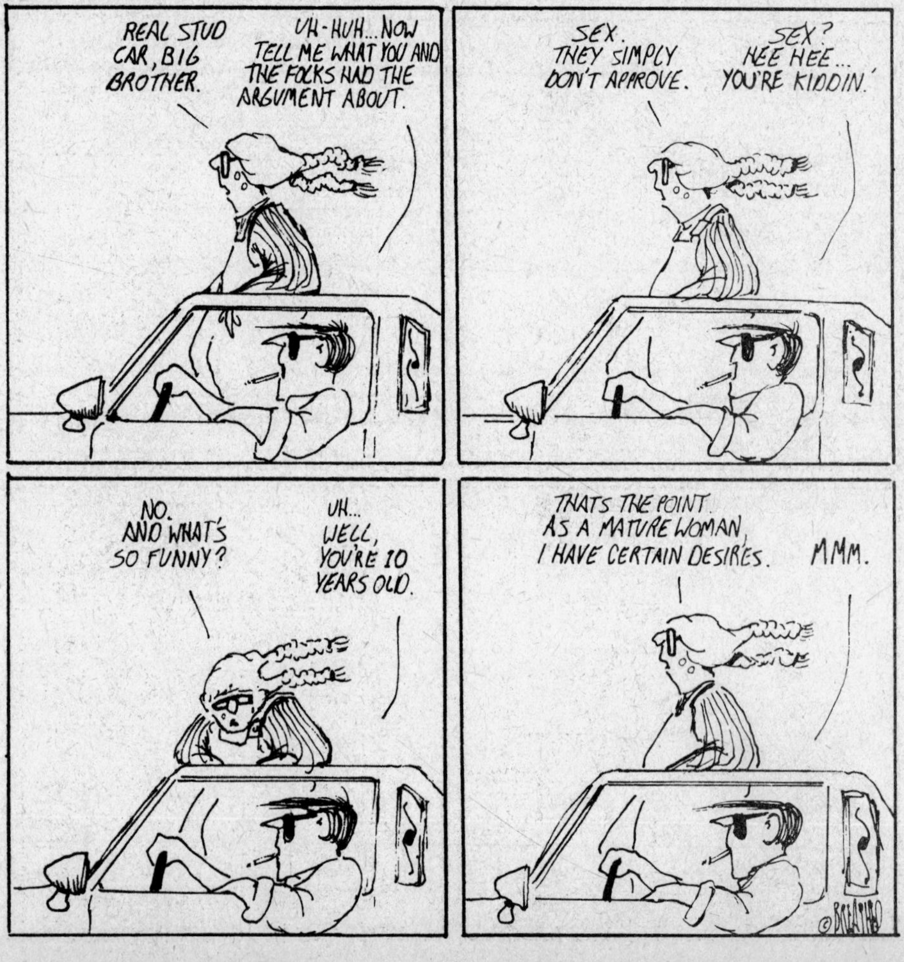
REAL STUD CAR, BIG BROTHER.
UH-HUH... NOW TELL ME WHAT YOU AND THE FOLKS HAD THE ARGUMENT ABOUT.
SEX. THEY SIMPLY DON'T APPROVE.
SEX? HEE HEE... YOU'RE KIDDIN'.
NO. AND WHAT'S SO FUNNY?
UH... WELL, YOU'RE 10 YEARS OLD.
THATS THE POINT. AS A MATURE WOMAN, I HAVE CERTAIN DESIRES.
MMM.
© BREATHED

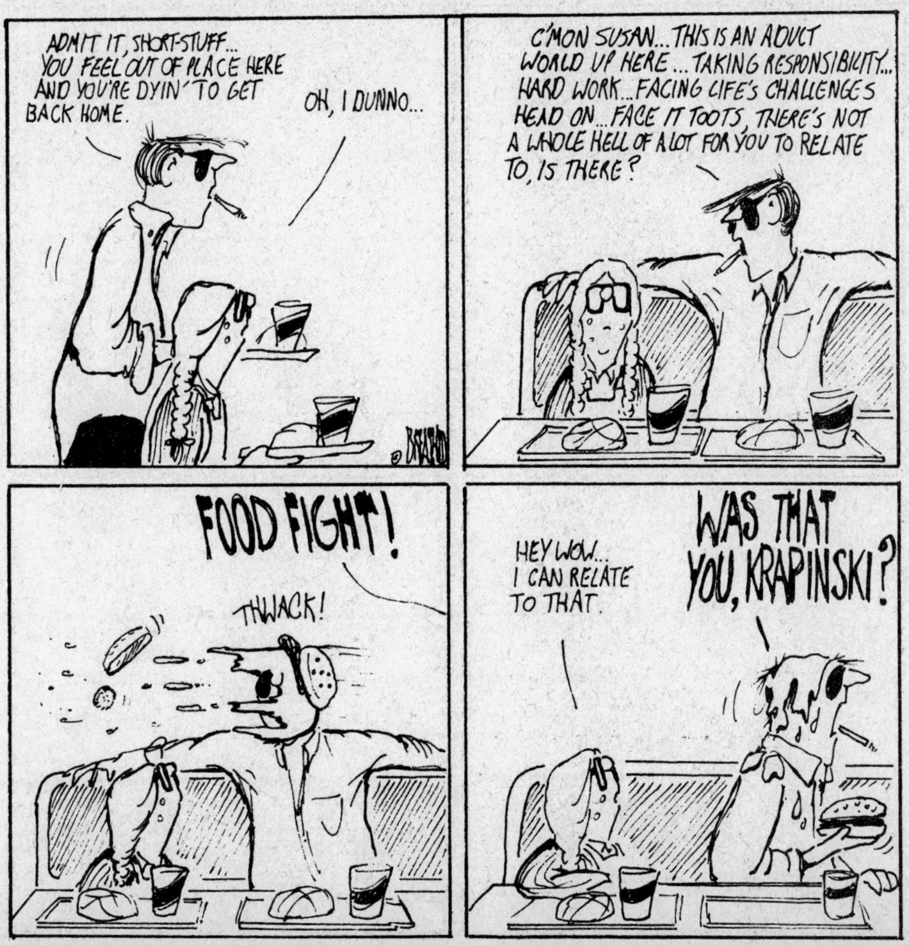
ADMIT IT, SHORT-STUFF... YOU FEEL OUT OF PLACE HERE AND YOU'RE DYIN' TO GET BACK HOME.
OH, I DUNNO...
© BREATHED
C'MON SUSAN... THIS IS AN ADULT WORLD UP HERE... TAKING RESPONSIBILITY... HARD WORK... FACING LIFE'S CHALLENGES HEAD ON... FACE IT TOOTS, THERE'S NOT A WHOLE HELL OF A LOT FOR YOU TO RELATE TO, IS THERE?
FOOD FIGHT!
THWACK!
HEY WOW... I CAN RELATE TO THAT.
WAS THAT YOU, KRAPINSKI?

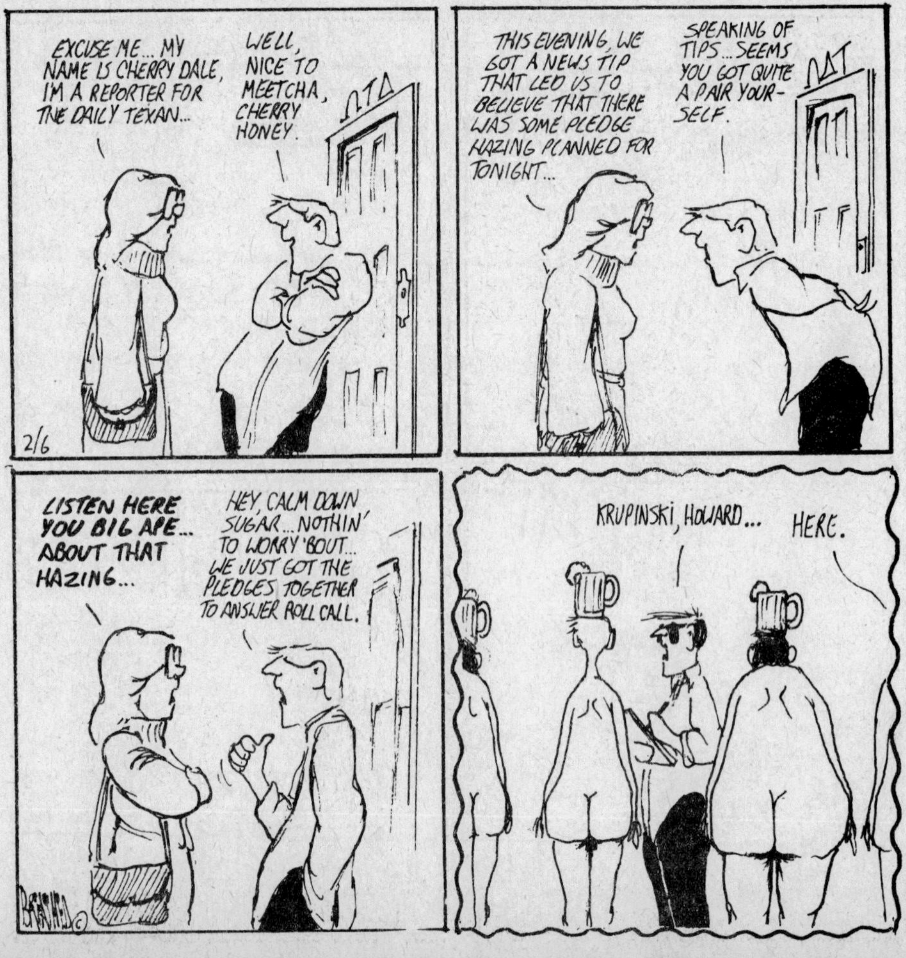
EXCUSE ME... MY NAME IS CHERRY DALE, I'M A REPORTER FOR THE DAILY TEXAN...
WELL, NICE TO MEETCHA, CHERRY HONEY.
2/6
THIS EVENING, WE GOT A NEWS TIP THAT LED US TO BELIEVE THAT THERE WAS SOME PLEDGE HAZING PLANNED FOR TONIGHT...
SPEAKING OF TIPS... SEEMS YOU GOT QUITE A PAIR YOURSELF.
LISTEN HERE YOU BIG APE... ABOUT THAT HAZING...
HEY, CALM DOWN SUGAR... NOTHIN' TO WORRY 'BOUT... WE JUST GOT THE PLEDGES TOGETHER TO ANSWER ROLL CALL.
KRUPINSKI, HOWARD...
HERE.

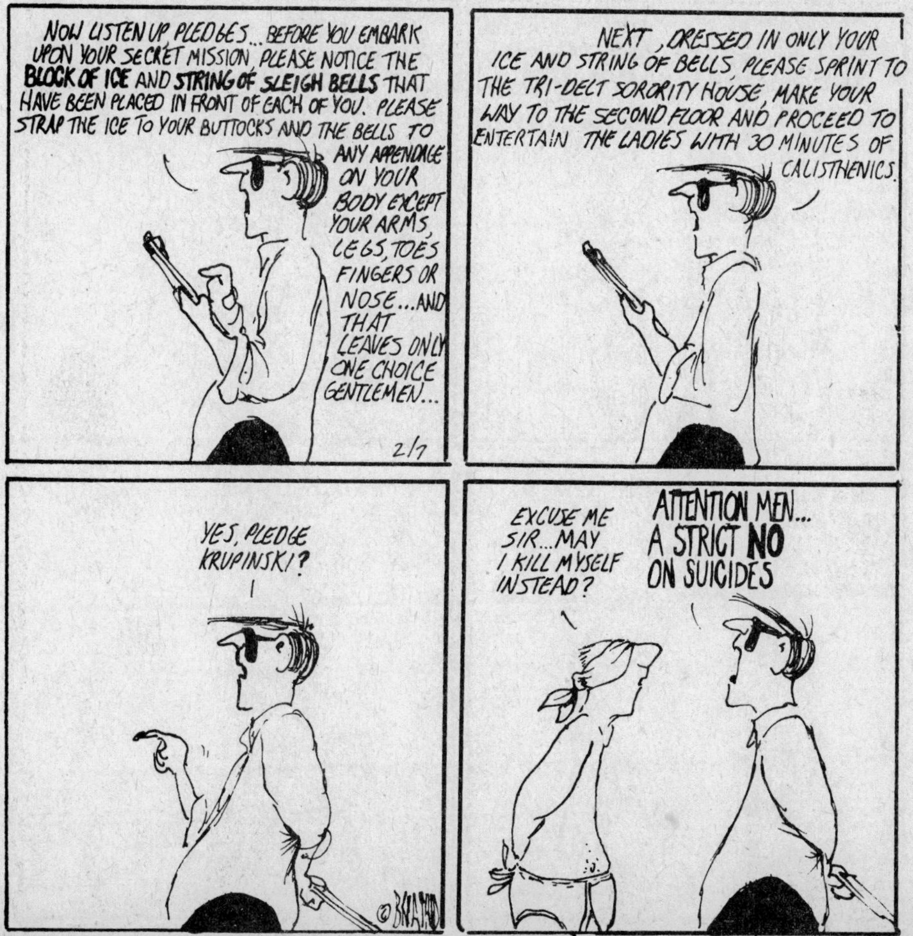
NOW LISTEN UP, PLEDGES... BEFORE YOU EMBARK UPON YOUR SECRET MISSION, PLEASE NOTICE THE BLOCK OF ICE AND STRING OF SLEIGH BELLS THAT HAVE BEEN PLACED IN FRONT OF EACH OF YOU. PLEASE STRAP THE ICE TO YOUR BUTTOCKS AND THE BELLS TO ANY APPENDAGE ON YOUR BODY EXCEPT YOUR ARMS, LEGS, TOES FINGERS OR NOSE... AND THAT LEAVES ONLY ONE CHOICE GENTLEMEN...
2/7
NEXT, DRESSED IN ONLY YOUR ICE AND STRING OF BELLS, PLEASE SPRINT TO THE TRI-DELT SORORITY HOUSE, MAKE YOUR WAY TO THE SECOND FLOOR AND PROCEED TO ENTERTAIN THE LADIES WITH 30 MINUTES OF CALISTHENICS.
YES, PLEDGE KRUPINSKI?
© BREATHED
EXCUSE ME SIR... MAY I KILL MYSELF INSTEAD?
ATTENTION MEN... A STRICT NO ON SUICIDES

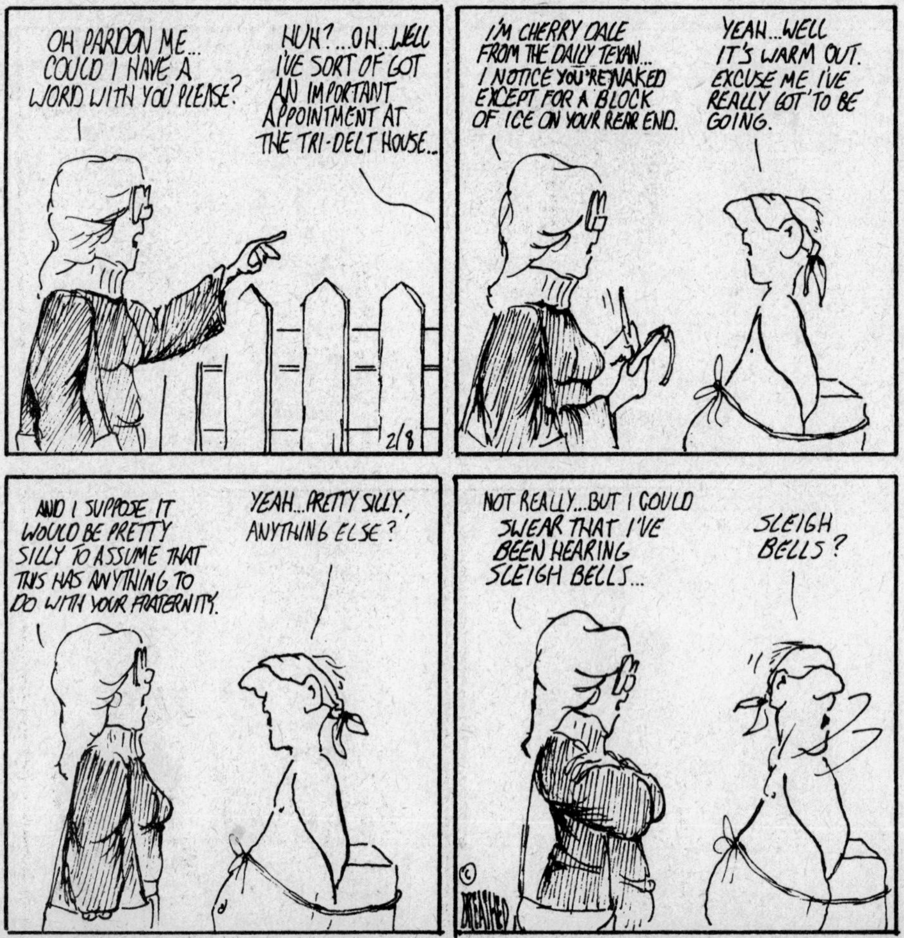
OH PARDON ME... COULD I HAVE A WORD WITH YOU PLEASE?
HUH?...OH...WELL I'VE SORT OF GOT AN IMPORTANT APPOINTMENT AT THE TRI-DELT HOUSE...
2/8
I'M CHERRY DALE FROM THE DAILY TEXAN... I NOTICE YOU'RE NAKED EXCEPT FOR A BLOCK OF ICE ON YOUR REAR END.
YEAH...WELL IT'S WARM OUT. EXCUSE ME I'VE REALLY GOT TO BE GOING.
AND I SUPPOSE IT WOULD BE PRETTY SILLY TO ASSUME THAT THIS HAS ANYTHING TO DO WITH YOUR FRATERNITY.
YEAH...PRETTY SILLY. ANYTHING ELSE?
NOT REALLY...BUT I COULD SWEAR THAT I'VE BEEN HEARING SLEIGH BELLS...
SLEIGH BELLS?

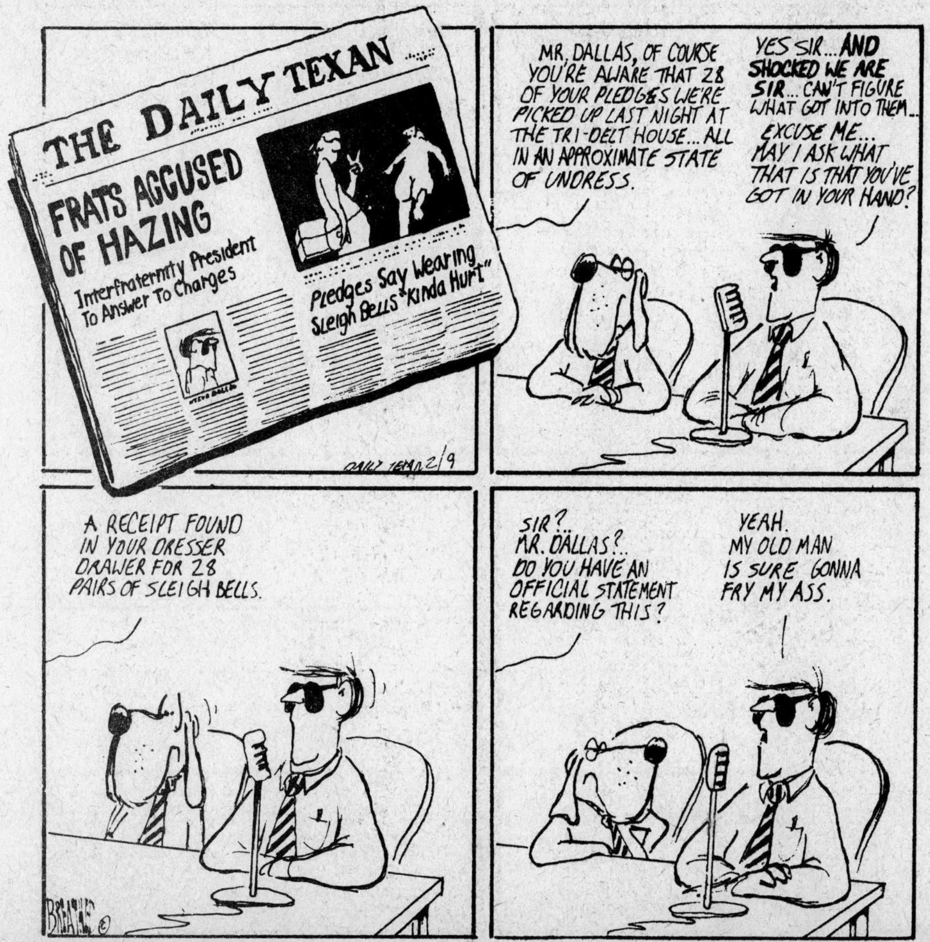
THE DAILY TEXAN
FRATS ACCUSED OF HAZING
Interfraternity President To Answer To Charges
Pledges Say Wearing Sleigh Bells "Kinda Hurt"
MR. DALLAS, OF COURSE YOU'RE AWARE THAT 28 OF YOUR PLEDGES WERE PICKED UP LAST NIGHT AT THE TRI-DELT HOUSE... ALL IN AN APPROXIMATE STATE OF UNDRESS.
YES SIR... AND SHOCKED WE ARE SIR... CAN'T FIGURE WHAT GOT INTO THEM...
EXCUSE ME... MAY I ASK WHAT THAT IS THAT YOU'VE GOT IN YOUR HAND?
A RECEIPT FOUND IN YOUR DRESSER DRAWER FOR 28 PAIRS OF SLEIGH BELLS.
SIR?... MR. DALLAS?... DO YOU HAVE AN OFFICIAL STATEMENT REGARDING THIS?
YEAH. MY OLD MAN IS SURE GONNA FRY MY ASS.

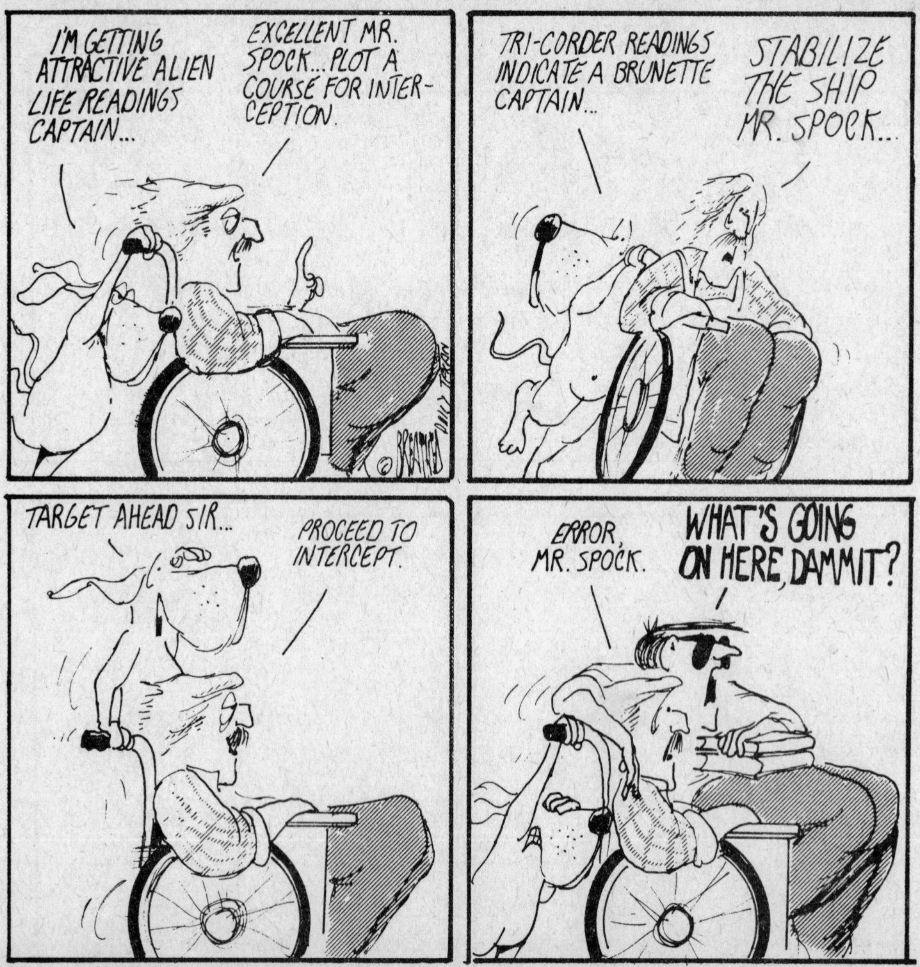

I'M GETTING ATTRACTIVE ALIEN LIFE READINGS CAPTAIN...
EXCELLENT MR. SPOCK...PLOT A COURSE FOR INTER-CEPTION.
TRI-CORDER READINGS INDICATE A BRUNETTE CAPTAIN...
STABILIZE THE SHIP MR. SPOCK...
TARGET AHEAD SIR...
PROCEED TO INTERCEPT.
ERROR, MR. SPOCK.
WHAT'S GOING ON HERE, DAMMIT?